Hearing God's Voice
For Yourself

Hearing God's Voice For Yourself

A Beginner's Guide

Marilyn Parmelee

To order additional copies of this book, contact:
Xlibris Corporation
1-888-795-4274
www.Xlibris.com
Orders@Xlibris.com
47164

CONTENTS

Section Five: Practicing The Prophetic

FORWARD

Before I was asked to write the forward to this book, I was asked to comment on it. As I attempted to do so, I found myself utilizing the information and principles from it in my ministry, rather than commenting on it, I was gleaning from it. Rather than being a friend offering my opinions, I became a student absorbed with the rich teachings this book offers.

Three areas of this book particularly stood out to me: God Communicates Through Dreams and Visions, Mystical Christianity (of which I cannot wait for Marilyn to write more about), and the exercises for awareness and prophetic development.

I believe for all those that are beginners in the prophetic and seasoned prophetic ministers will find this an excellent resource for learning and developing a daily spiritual discipline.

I cannot wait for my dear friend Pastor Marilyn to write the sequel to this work (especially touching on the Mystics). I have suggested she develop accompanying journals and study guides along with the rich text she puts forth.

Pastor Marilyn I believe this is just the beginning of what God has called you into. I feel that many spiritual sons and daughters will be birthed from this book. With true sincerity, I believe you are a mother in Israel, like Deborah of old, who judged (taught) Israel.

Love, Your Brother
Prophet Lauro R. Adame

INTRODUCTION

One day I was watching a television talk show and the guest was a woman who called herself an intuitive. She was talking about a book she had written that would help people develop their intuition. I was curious because the methods she talked about were similar to the ones that God had taught me over the years to develop my spirit. I went and purchased the book just to see if that wasn't what she was, in essence, doing. It was! This was a woman who had learned how to develop her spirit, but unfortunately, because she was not using biblical checks and balances she was leaving herself and her reader open to hearing not just God's Spirit, but other spirits as well.

I asked God, "Where is your simple book on developing our human spirit and operating in the prophetic?" He said, "Yes Marilyn, where is it?" That day I began to seriously study the prophetic, to study about what is needed to hear God speak and to develop our spirit, our discernment of what is God and what is not.

Not only have I studied the Bible and other books on this issue, but since 1995 I also have been privileged to attend the meetings of one of the greatest prophets of our time, Prophet Kim Clement. I have also been privileged to attend meetings the Kim Clement has hosted called, "Training for Staining" where we learned from different prophets and prophetic people how to hear God's voice.

This is not a book for people who are consistently hearing Gods voice and operating in the prophetic. It is for beginners. It is my hope, my prayer that this book will help you on your journey to hear God, first for yourself and then for others. May God bless you on your journey.

SECTION ONE

Foundations

CHAPTER ONE

FOUNDATIONS OVERVIEW

When I speak of hearing God's voice, I am speaking of learning how to communicate with God and how He communicates with us. In order to begin to communicate with God effectively, there are some foundational truths that need to be in place.

Foundation One: Created By God

Scripture tells us we were created to know God, to be a friend of His and to walk and talk with Him face to face. We have been made in His image and likeness. We have been made to rule and to reign with Him for eternity. At one time, God even walked and talked with man in the Garden of Eden. When man fell through committing treason against God, He already had a plan to restore man into his rightful place.

Think about this with me for just a minute. God yearned for someone to talk to, someone to have companionship with, and someone to work with. So, He made a companion for Himself. Today, He still longs for someone who loves Him and wants to be with Him as much as He wants to be with them. However, it is impossible to be that someone if you don't know Him.

For this reason, God sent His Son Jesus as the way to bring reconciliation between Himself and man. In the book of John, chapter three in the Bible, we see that God sent His Son because He loved us and wanted us to be reconciled to Him. All we have to do is believe that God made this sacrifice for us, and to accept this sacrifice. Once we accept Jesus as that sacrifice, we are restored into the family of God as His children.

Scriptures tell us what Jesus did for us. God the Son was born of a virgin to become a man, Jesus. He lived a sinless life and became the perfect sacrifice, and chose to die for us on a cross. Not only did He die, but He then came alive again and is still alive today. Not only can we be restored to right fellowship with God, we have also been given the power to become the sons of God. When we accept Jesus as Savior, we become God's children, literally a son of God.

Have you been reconciled to God? Do you want to be? If you do, in your own words, ask Him. Let Him know that you accept the sacrifice of His Son for you, and that you want to be reconciled to Him. You do not have to pray a special prayer. Just speak to Him from your heart. Once you have done that, whether you "feel" anything or not, you are forgiven and reconciled to Him. You have been reconciled by accepting God's sacrifice of Jesus for you. If you could have been reconciled any other way, Jesus would not have had to die for you. So accept what Jesus did, and ask God to reconcile you to Himself on the basis of what Jesus did.

After we have been reconciled to God, it is then important that we begin to develop our relationship with Him. All of the exercises given in this book are designed to help you do that.

Scripture References:
Genesis 1:26 through 3:24
John 1:1-18
John chapters 19-20
2 Corinthians 5:17-21
2 Peter 1:1-4

Foundation Two: Created In His Image

"All that the Father is, we see revealed in the Son; all that is the Son's is the Father's also; for the whole Son dwells in the Father, and He has the whole Father dwelling in Himself . . . The Son who exists always in the Father can never be separated from Him, nor can the Spirit ever be divided from the Son who through the Spirit works all things. He who receives the Father also receives at the same time the Son and the Spirit. It is impossible to envisage any kind of severance or disjunction

between them: One cannot think of the Son apart from the Father, nor divide the Spirit from the Son. There is between the three a sharing and a differentiation that are beyond words and understanding."

"The distinction between the persons does not impair the oneness of nature, nor does the shared unity of essence lead to confusion between the distinctive characteristics of the persons. Do not be surprised that we should speak of the Godhead as being at the same time both unified and differentiated. Using riddles, as it were, we envisage a strange and paradoxical diversity-in-unity and unity-in-diversity." Gregory of Nyssa, Unity In Diversity.

We are three, yet we are one. If you slap my face, you will physically hurt my body, you will hurt my feelings, and you will wound my spirit. I am one—but I have three levels of being. God is one, but He has three levels of being. He is God the Father, (mind, will and emotions), God the Son, (body), and God the Holy Spirit, (spirit). You can speak of the different levels, but you cannot separate the person of God because He is one. Just as God has a spirit, a soul, and a body, so do we as well. We are triune beings. We are a spirit, we have a soul, and we live in a body. With our spirit, we contact the spiritual realm, and with it we can be in contact with God Almighty. With our soul, we contact the intellectual realm, and it holds our will, emotions, imagination, and memory. Scriptures tell us that only the Word of God can separate our spirit and soul. With our body, we contact the physical realm by using our senses.

1 Thessalonians 5:23 tells us that he prays our whole spirit, soul, and body be preserved blameless at the coming of our Lord. Our spirit is who we are. Our soul is our mind, our will and our emotions. Our body is what houses our spirit and our soul. Study this out further in the Scriptures if this is unfamiliar to you, for there is no substitute for a personal knowledge of the person of God.

Spirit—Your spirit is the "real" you.

Romans 8:1, 4-7
1 Corinthians 6:20
Galatians 5:16-25; 6:8
Ephesians 2:22; 3:16; 4:23
Hebrews 4:12
James 2:26

Soul—The will, emotions, intellect, imagination, and memory. The will is where we choose to resist or receive this information. It is where we enforce our beliefs, and the decisions we make. God gave our emotions to us, and contrary to some teachings, they are a good thing. We just don't make our decisions based on emotion. Our emotions are one of the main ways we give other spirits access to our souls. Our intellect is where we analyze and reason. Our imagination can be either productive or nonproductive. We use our imagination to meditate and think on the things of God, or on nonproductive vain things. We make the decision on how it is to be used. Let your imagination be a good thing. Lastly, our memories hold our thoughts, and feelings from past experiences.

1 Chronicles 29:18 (KJV)
Hebrews 4:12
1 Peter 2:11
3 John 2

Body—Our physical senses, sight, hearing, smell, taste, and touch. Your physical body is the house or earth suit for your spirit. It does what you tell it to. It has wants, desires, and needs, but the decisions are made through your spirit and soul. Guard your senses, because they are the entrances to your human body.

Romans 8:11, 13-14, 23
1 Corinthians 6:20; 9:27; 15:20-31
James 3:2-6

You will be using exercises in this book to develop your spirit. Developing your spirit will cause your soul and body to begin to line up with the Word of God.

Foundation Three: Being Baptized In The Spirit

If being baptized in the Holy Spirit is new to you, look up and read the following Scriptures:

Acts 1:5
Acts 2:4, 38
Acts 8:15

Acts 10:38; 44-48
Acts 11:16
Acts 19:6
1 John 5:14, 15

We need the baptism of the Holy Spirit. Jesus showed us how to walk on this earth as a spirit-filled human being. He promised us that when He left He would send the Holy Spirit to us. He said that the Holy Spirit would bear witness with our spirits, that He would guide us to all truth, and He would help us to pray.

Once we've been reconciled to God, in order to receive the Holy Spirit, we need only to ask. We should not be afraid, because it is God we are receiving. Just as we use our voice, our mouth, and our tongue to talk in our natural language, we must also use them to speak in our spiritual language. So, go ahead, just ask.

Example Of Prayer:

"Father, in the name of Jesus, I thank you for reconciling me to Yourself and cleansing me of all unrighteousness. Jesus promised me a gift, the baptism of the Holy Spirit. I ask You, Lord, to baptize me with Your Spirit. Help me that I may speak with other tongues."

Now that you have been baptized in the Holy Spirit pray in other tongues.

Foundation Four: Develop A Relationship With God

We develop our relationship with God by reading the Scriptures, by developing our prayer life, and by meditating on His Word. There will be exercises throughout this book to help you develop your relationship with God.

Foundation Five: A Spiritual Mentor

The mentor you choose should be someone who knows God, knows God's voice and will help you evaluate whether what you are getting is from God or not. When we are first learning, we need the input of others. It could be your pastor or some other mature Christian in your church. Our safeguards, as we learn to hear God's voice for ourselves, are knowledge of Scripture, prayer, and godly counsel.

Foundation Six: Overview Of The Ways God Communicates

One of the most amazing things about being a Christian is that God Himself wants to talk to us. He wants to have a relationship with us, His creation. There are many ways He talks to us, and I'm going to give you a little overview of that now. We will go more in-depth on each one in later chapters.

God speaks to us through the Scriptures, both through reading and studying the Bible and through praying the Scriptures. This is one of the main ways He speaks to us today.

God also speaks to us through the counsel of others. Mature Christians can help you, but what they say should confirm what God is telling you already. If you are new to Christianity, they can help you discern what God is saying to you.

God will also use common sense to guide and direct you. Read 1 Thessalonians 3:1, 2. We need to pray about everything, but God doesn't expect our common sense to stop.

God can speak to us through circumstances and creation as well as things. God moves in the natural. We need to get over our idea that we need to be super spiritual to hear God's voice. He has many ways of speaking to us, and we must always be looking and keeping an atmosphere of listening, just as a parent keeps their ear open to listen for their child's voice.

God can speak to us through our memories, triggered in any number of ways. It could be a phrase that comes to mind or a verse of Scripture. It could be a song we keep hearing, or a conversation we've had with someone. It could be a picture of a scene, or a scent, or odor. Don't rule out your memories.

God also speaks to us through our conscience. People will say something like, "I heard my mind say . . ."

God speaks to us through the Holy Spirit speaking to our spirit. These will be spontaneous thoughts and impressions that flow from the Holy Spirit to our spirit, going directly to our mind where they are registered. He speaks to us through an inward knowing, through an inward witness, and through an inward voice. He speaks to us through the voice of the Holy Spirit. It will seem to be a hunch or "gut feeling", a basic insight, or just knowing a general direction to go in.

God also speaks to us today in dreams. He even speaks to us in visions. He speaks in an audible voice. You may have heard it yourself and didn't even realize it.

God also speaks to us through the gifts of the Holy Spirit. These are through prophetic words, a word of knowledge, a word of wisdom, and through the discerning of spirits.

We will be looking at the different ways God speaks to us, as well as exercises you can do to develop your ability to hear as we go along in the book.

Let's begin our journey now!

CHAPTER TWO

KNOWING GOD

The most frequently asked question I get as a pastor is, "How can I hear God's voice"? The answer is simple but not easy. You must get to know God. If you do not know Him you will never know if it is really God talking to you or not. Getting to know God is a privilege we have as His children. We get to know Him the same way we get to know anyone else; we spend time with Him. We read the Scriptures so we know what He has to say about Himself, and spend time in prayer, talking to Him. Now, instead of going on and on about what you need to do, I'm going to give you some exercises that will help you. I've always hated it when people tell me what to do but not how to do it. So here we go. Are you ready?

First of all, get out a notebook and pencil or pen. I prefer erasable pens. You will be writing a lot. I'd like you to use a notebook (a three-ring binder) so that you can put all your answers to the exercises in it for the duration of this book. This is your journal and you will be referring back to it from time to time.

Now, here are a few things you can do. I suggest trying all of them and then sticking with the ones you like best.

Exercise One

1. Sit or stand in a comfortable position.
2. Play soft instrumental music.
3. Take a few deep breaths.

4. Think on a portion of Scripture.
5. If your mind wanders, write down what is on your mind. Go right back to thinking on the Scripture.
6. Sit in silence before Him, just to be in His presence.

Exercise Two

1. Pick a passage of Scripture that expresses to Him how you feel.
2. Read it to Him.
3. Be silent before Him.
4. Write down anything that comes to your mind.

Exercise Three

1. Write God a poem that expresses to Him how you feel about Him.
2. Read it to Him.
3. Be silent before Him.
4. Write down anything that comes to your mind.

Example From My Journal:

"Hi Jesus. Just wanted to say I love You. I've talked about You a lot today but I've just talked to You a little bit, big difference. I've told everyone else so now I'll tell You.
You are wonderful
You're always there
You always care
Your plan is sure without a flaw
Ours is a relationship of the heart
So we're never apart
Your presence is with me throughout the day
You never walk away
You hold me whenever I'm sad or afraid
And when I cry You wipe my tears away
You're the only one I can count on
You are more than enough."

As you can see, it doesn't have to be professional or polished. You are just expressing yourself to the God whom you love.

Exercise Four

1.   Start a book of prayers.
2.   Write out your prayers to Him.
3.   Date them.
4.   Read them to Him.
5.   Record the date on them when you receive your answer.

Exercise Five

1.   Start a Book of Remembrance. God keeps a Book of Remembrance about us, so why not keep one on Him?
2.   Include things that He has done for you that made you feel special.
3.   Things that you are grateful for.
4.   You can include pictures of the things God has given you, like you would for a family album or scrapbook.

Example From My Journal:

"Oh Lord the times we've shared! There really is no one like You. I just went back, reading the moments we've had together, so nice to have a record of them, so many left out."

"One event was especially precious to me. On a Monday in Idaho, You met with me, mingled with me. Your love and compassion filled me and surrounded me. Every time I think of it I still feel it. It causes such emotion in me; it's so intense it causes tears to come to my eyes. That experience has helped me more times than I can remember. Your love always gets me through whatever I have to go through. Just wanted to let You know."

Exercise Six

1.   Sing a love song to Him.
2.   Just enjoy His presence.

Exercise Seven

1.   Write down a question that you would like God to answer for you. Be specific.

2. Each day for a week, read a portion of Scripture. Read until He stops you. Write down what He has shared with you.
3. At the end of the week, go over it. Has He answered your question?

Example From My Journal:

"Question: Jesus, You and Your disciples took the time needed to minister to the people. We will do the same. Where do we start?"

"Answer: *As you begin to minister, minister to what you can see and what you know. As you do, I will add what you don't know.*"

Thank you Jesus!

CHAPTER THREE

LEARNING TO DISCERN

To discern means to distinguish between, to detect, to discriminate, or to come to know. Scriptures tell us that we must learn to discern between good and evil. It is our job and it takes practice. Look in Hebrews 5:14 It says, " . . . *but solid food is for the mature, for those whose faculties have been trained by practice to distinguish good from evil.*" So it takes practice. Don't be too hard on yourself if you don't know if something is God or not. It really takes practice, and your spiritual mentor can help you through the early learning stages. The following is a list of other Scriptures to help you understand discernment:

Romans 12:2 (transformed by the renewing of your mind)
1 John 4:1-6 (test the spirits)
Hebrews 3:7-15; 4:12; 5:14; 6:1 (Word discerns the thoughts and intents of the heart)

As children of God it is our right and our responsibility to hear God's voice, and to follow what He is telling us to do. Jesus modeled this for us. He came as a human being, walked as a human filled with the Holy Spirit and it says He only did those things which He saw the Father do. That is how we are supposed to be. It is imperative that we walk and talk like Jesus did; a human filled with the Holy Spirit doing only those things which we see the Father doing. In order to do this, our discernment must be developed. The way we develop our discernment is through reading, praying, and meditating on the Scriptures. In the next chapter, we will be going into those things in more detail.

We also need to put the word of God into practice in our lives, not only reading and hearing the Word, but acting upon it as well. Until we do something, we really don't fully understand it. Worship also helps us to become familiar with God and to be able to discern what is from Him and what is not. These things help us to train our human spirit in the ways of God, so that when we perceive something by the spirit, we can act on it immediately as Jesus did.

Because we have been reconciled to God, we have been born into the Kingdom of God. We have been given His divine nature. Again, we are a spirit, we have a soul, and we live in a body. All of us need to be trained in the ways of the kingdom. It is important to know that God will never tell you do something that is contrary to Scripture. If it is not covered in the Scriptures, it will line up with what the Scriptures say and with the character of God. That's one of the reasons that reading and meditating on the Scriptures are so important.

On the following page, you will find a sheet that will help you learn how to know if something is you, if it is God or if it is another spirit trying to influence you. You may want a copy to keep in your notebook in order to refer to it easily. You have my permission to do so for your own use.

TESTING WHAT YOU'RE GETTING

(Images, Thoughts, Impressions)

When asking God for His leading, these are areas we need to be especially cautious. Check to see if the word or guidance you receive is any of the following:

- ☐ Something you intensely desire.
- ☐ Something you really don't want to happen.
- ☐ Anything that is a substitute for an intimate relationship with God.
- ☐ Something that lifts up you, not God.

Adapted from "How To Hear God's Voice" by Mark and Patti Virkler
Available at www.cwgministries.org
(used with permission)

Find It's Origin, Test It's Content & Check It's Fruit 1 John 4:1,5; Matthew 7:16

SELF	GOD	ANOTHER SPIRIT
Comes from the mind/a progressive building of ideas. My wants, desires, & thoughts.	Pictures and thoughts come from the inner— most being. Sensed in spirit, then formed.	Comes from the mind. A picture or thought.
May be good or bad. Consideration of things I have learned. May or may not want to test it.	Instructive, uplifting, comforting & peaceful. Not afraid of testing.	Negative, destructive, pushy, fearful, anxious, unsettled, exhaustion, condemnation. Afraid of being tested.
Results vary.	Quickens faith, peace, good fruit, knowledge, enlightenment, strength & humility.	Fear, compulsion, bondage, anxiety, confusion, inflated ego.

SECTION TWO

The Ways God Communicates

CHAPTER FOUR

GOD COMMUNICATES THROUGH

THE SCRIPTURES

As I've said before, one of the questions I am asked most often is, "How can I hear the voice of God for myself"? So what I am going to share with you is how I learned to hear God's voice. I am going to share with you some books that God used to teach me, along with the Bible. There are three books that have probably been the biggest influence on my life. The first one was written by Evelyn Christiansen, "Lord Change Me!" The second is by Benny Hinn, "Good Morning Holy Spirit." The third is by Madame Guyon, "Experiencing God through Prayer".

The one thing that I didn't understand when I first got saved, or even when I first got filled with the Holy Spirit, is how God talks to people. I knew that He talked to us through the Scriptures and through prayer. I also knew that our conscience guided us. But I discovered that He speaks to us in so many other ways!

We must understand how God talks to us and how He sounds, if you will, so that we know when it's God, when it's another spirit and when it is us. That's very important to know. We need to be able to learn how to discern that for ourselves. I want you to understand that it is going to take practice. It's going to take doing the exercises in this book and putting them into practice in your life on a regular basis. One of the things that we should be able to do, as a Christian, is to be able to hear from God and put into practice what He is saying to us. And sometimes it is simply reading a passage of Scripture where there is a command, and doing it. So what I want you to learn is how to take the Scriptures and get something from God for yourself, and be able to use it in your life.

God Speaks Through Reading The Scriptures

I first learned how to really hear God through the Scriptures after reading the book, "Lord Change Me!" by Evelyn Christiansen. I'm just going to quote this passage to you, from pages 46 and 47. *"From that day on, we let God be in command. I assigned a portion of Scripture instructing them to take this portion of Scripture, find any spot in this cabin and read until God speaks to you. Read only until he speaks to you. Don't read any more. If you read after he speaks you'll get confused not knowing what you should pray about. Then ask God why he stopped you at this point, what needs changing in your life, and then what he wants you to do about it."*

When you're reading Scripture, not studying, but just when you are reading, read until something stands out to you. For instance, let's go to Psalm 120 and we'll start in verse 1. *"In my distress I cried out to the Lord, and he heard me. Deliver my soul, O Lord; from lying lips and from a deceitful tongue. What shall be given to you, or what shall be done to you, you false tongue? Sharp arrows of the warrior, with coals of the broom tree! Woe is me that I dwell in Meshech. That I dwell among the tents of Kedar! My soul has dwelt too long with one who hates peace. I am for peace; but when I speak, they are for war."*

Now I would keep reading in chapter 121 because nothing has spoken to me yet. *"I will lift up my eyes to the hills from whence comes my help? My help comes from the Lord, who made heaven and earth."* Now that speaks to me. My help comes from the Lord, who made heaven and earth. And so, I would write that down. I would put a date on the paper. The next day, I would either keep reading in Psalms, or go somewhere else if I felt the Lord wanted me to. I would do this for about a week. Then at the end of the week I would go back and look and see what God had spoken to me that week, because this is God speaking to me through the Scriptures.

It is not that you are just picking something out of Scriptures and making it say what you want to make it say. It is God speaking to you. He quickens it to your spirit. He causes you to pay attention to it, so write it down and date it. I have made forms for this that can be found at the end of this chapter for you to copy for your personal use, or to just use them for a guide in your notebook. I call the form "Daily Spiritual Practice". I got the idea from Tim LaHaye's book, "How to Study the Bible for Yourself".

Reading The Scriptures Exercise

Now try it yourself. Grab your Bible. Get out your notebook and a pencil or pen. Ask the Holy Spirit to lead you, guide you and direct you as you read. Ask Him to help you understand what you read. Ask Him to teach you. Ask Him to remove any preconceived ideas you may have.

Pick a passage of Scripture to start with. Read only until God speaks. A verse or even just a word will stand out to you. Stop there. Write out the passage of Scripture(s). Analyze why the Lord stopped you at that point. Does it answer a question you've asked? How does it apply to your life? Is it a command? Is it a principle? Can you act on it now? Repeat this practice on a daily basis for one week. At the end of the week, go through your notes. What has the Lord said to you this week through the Scriptures? What principles has He taught you? What in His Word have you begun to act on?

God Speaks Through Praying The Scriptures

This truth I learned from Madame Guyon's book, "Experiencing God through Prayer". For example, take the Scripture in Psalm 121 we read earlier. You can pray it back to Him, *"Father God I thank You that my help comes from You, who has made the heavens and the earth."* One of the things this will do for you is to help you incorporate a greater knowledge of who God is in your life. The Scriptures will become a part of you. It will also help you in meditation, which we will be discussing shortly.

Praying The Scriptures Exercise

Before you begin, get out your notebook, a pencil or pen and your Bible. If while you are spending this time with the Lord you have thoughts that try to intrude, write them down so that your mind will be at ease.

Ask the Holy Spirit to direct you to a passage of Scripture. If you don't feel led to a particular Scripture passage, choose a Psalm or a Proverb. Next, begin to read the passage of Scripture. Don't hurry through it. Read it slowly. You don't want to move from one passage to another, not until you have sensed the essence of what you have read. Read until the Holy Spirit touches you. Stop there and turn it into prayer.

You will find a form you can copy for your personal use at the end of this chapter. Or you can just use it as a guide in your notebook.

God Speaks Through Meditating On The Scriptures

Meditation is a scriptural concept. Joshua 1:8 tells us to meditate on the Word of God day and night. You will not develop spiritual wisdom without meditating on the Scriptures. Meditation involves four things: thinking on, seeing, feeling and rehearsing over and over the scene you are meditating on. When we meditate we lay aside distractions and focus our soul, (mind, will and emotions) on the Scriptures. Meditation helps get the meaning of the Scriptures into us, making the truths a part of our lives, causing the Scriptures to leap off the page or just come to our attention spontaneously during the day as we need them. If you are not in the habit of meditating, I would suggest you start with just 15 minutes a day.

It is important that you understand that meditation is mentally imaging what God says, (1 Chronicles 29:18). Prophet Kim Clement has often said, "What you see, you be". Meditation is a key to seeing. As you meditate, mentally image God being with you in every situation as you go about your day, knowing that no matter what is happening He is there to help you.

Meditating On The Scripture Exercise

Before you begin, get your Bible, notebook and pencil or pen. If while you are meditating on the Scriptures you are distracted from something, notice it and bring your attention back to the Scripture. If it is something you must do, write it down, and then bring your attention back to the Scripture.

Ask the Holy Spirit to direct you as you meditate. Pick a passage of Scripture and begin to read. Read until the Holy Spirit stops you. Read it again. Imagine yourself in the setting of this Scripture. See if you can smell the smells, feel what is happening. Involve all your senses as you meditate. Think about the Scripture. What is God showing you?

After you have finished meditating, write out what God has shown you. There is a form to guide you at the end of this chapter.

Practice This Exercise For A Week

After you've tried doing each exercise one time, do one each day for a week to get the feel of how this allows you to hear God's voice. At the end of the week, look through your sheets and use the form at the end of this chapter to see what God has been saying to you this week.

Practice This Exercise For Three Weeks

Okay, now that we've asked God to speak to us through the Scriptures for a week let's challenge ourselves to hear God by asking Him some specific questions. Get out a pencil, paper and three envelopes.

1. Choose one of the following groups of three questions on three separate pieces of paper.

    ❑ How do You feel about me?
    ❑ What can I do to know You better?
    ❑ What gifts have You placed in me?

    ❑ How do You feel about sinners?
    ❑ How do You feel about sin?
    ❑ How can I best witness to others about You?

2. Now follow these instructions.

    ❑ Fold the pieces of paper so that the writing does not show.
    ❑ Place each slip of paper in a separate envelope.
    ❑ Seal the envelopes.
    ❑ Mix them up.
    ❑ Number each one.
    ❑ Put the sealed envelopes in a pocket in your notebook.

3. Now on the following days do the following. (Remember to record your answers each day.)

☐ Monday, envelope one, ask God to speak to you through the Scriptures regarding this question.

☐ Tuesday, envelope two, ask God to speak to you through the Scriptures regarding this question.

☐ Wednesday, envelope three, ask God to speak to you through the Scriptures regarding this question.

☐ Thursday, envelope two, ask God to speak to you through the Scriptures regarding this question.

☐ Friday, envelope three, ask God to speak to you through the Scriptures regarding this question.

☐ Saturday, envelope one, ask God to speak to you through the Scriptures regarding this question.

☐ At the end of each week, look at the answers you are getting for the questions in the envelopes. Use the weekly form as a guide. At the end of three weeks use the weekly form to see what God has said to you during the three weeks. What did you find out? Record your answers in your notebook, but do not open the envelopes! We will be using them again for a later exercise.

DAILY SPIRITUAL PRACTICE
READING THE WORD

Remember before you begin reading, ask the Holy Spirit to help you, direct you and guide you as you read.

Date: _____ Passage: _____

Read a portion of Scripture until the Holy Spirit stops you. Look for the following:

God's message to me today: _____

_____

_____

_____

Is this a promise from God? What is the promise? Is it a command? Is it a principle? How does it apply to me?

_____

_____

_____

Are there conditions? _____

_____

_____

_____

Additional comments: _____

_____

_____

_____

DAILY SPIRITUAL PRACTICE PRAYING THE WORD

Before you begin, get out your Bible, a notebook and pencil or pen. Keep them handy. If while you are spending this time with the Lord you have thoughts that try to intrude, write them down so that your mind can be at ease that it will be taken care of.

Ask the Holy Spirit to direct you to a passage of Scripture. If you don't feel led to a particular Scripture, choose a Psalm or Proverb. Next, begin to read the passage. Don't hurry through it. Read it slowly. You do not want to move from one passage to another, not until you have sensed the very heart of what you have read. Read until the Holy Spirit touches you. Stop there and turn it into prayer.

Date: _____ Passage: _____

Write out the Scripture passage: _____
_____
_____
_____
_____
_____

Now write out your prayer: _____
_____
_____
_____
_____
_____
_____
_____

DAILY SPIRITUAL PRACTICE
MEDITATING ON THE SCRIPTURES

Always before starting, ask the Holy Spirit to lead guide and direct you as you meditate. Choose your passage of Scripture you want to meditate on. Imagine yourself in the Scripture. See yourself there. Feel the textures of the clothing, the feelings they are feeling. Smell what they must be smelling. Hear the sounds. Become a part of the Scripture.

Date: _____ Passage: _____

What was going through your mind? _____

_____

_____

Was anything said to you directly? _____What was said? _____

_____

_____

What did you hear? _____

_____

What did you smell? _____

_____

What did you see? _____

_____

What did you feel? _____

_____

What did you taste? _____

_____

What did you learn? _____

_____

WEEKLY SPIRITUAL EXERCISE
PUTTING IT ALL TOGETHER

1. Look at all your notes from the exercises you did this week. The different exercises of reading, praying and meditating on Scripture.
2. What do all the Scriptures have in common?

    ❑ What overall themes emerge? Don't look simply for the obvious. Some can be quite inconspicuous. _____
    _____
    _____

    ❑ If they don't seem to go together, does this illuminate other things that you have wanted answers to? _____
    _____
    _____

    ❑ In what ways are they similar? _____
    _____
    _____

3. What do they tell you about what God is saying to you? What areas of your life is He speaking to? _____
    _____
    _____

4. Did this answer any questions you've had on your mind?
    _____
    _____
    _____
    _____

5. Did this bring up any new questions you'd like answers to?
    _____
    _____
    _____
    _____

CHAPTER FIVE

GOD COMMUNICATES SPIRIT TO SPIRIT

The inward witness is one way God's Spirit speaks to our spirit. Some people call this intuition or a "gut feeling". They feel like they just know whether they should do something or whether they need to wait on something. Kenneth Hagin likened it to a traffic light. Red is a strong feeling for stop, green a strong feeling for go and yellow for a feeling of caution or that you need more information.

The inward voice is another way we hear the Spirit of God. We hear what He is saying when the words go from our spirit to our mind. This is the same voice of conscience (our own spirit's voice) that I talked about in the overview. This is the voice that people also call their intuition. People will describe this as saying, "I heard my mind say . . ." It sounds like you, but it is God talking to you. The Holy Spirit speaks to us Spirit to spirit.

The voice of the Holy Spirit is another way He speaks to us. This always comes from inside of us, and it always lines up with the Scriptures. It sounds a bit more authoritative than our own spirit's voice.

Here are some scriptures to look up and read if this is new to you:
Romans 2:12
Romans 9:1
Hebrews 9:14
1 John 5:7

Let's do some exercises that will help us develop these three ways to hear God for ourselves. Remember now, Scripture has admonished us that good and evil is only discerned by exercising our senses.

For the inward witness, we will do the following exercises. Make sure you have your pencil and paper handy and that you add the results to your notebook.

Yes or No Exercise 1

- ❑ Think back to a time when you had to make a decision of whether or not to do something and you felt like you should. What did that feel like?
- ❑ Now think of a time when you felt the answer was no. What did that feel like?
- ❑ Now think of a time when you felt like the answer was to wait. What did that feel like?
- ❑ Record your answers in your notebook.

Yes or No Exercise 2

- ❑ Sit comfortably and take a few deep breaths to relax. This is not a test and you can't do it right or wrong.
- ❑ Take a moment to notice what sounds you are hearing, what you see around you, what you are feeling, tasting and sensing.
- ❑ Notice what is going through your mind.
- ❑ Now take another deep breath and let it all fade into the background.
- ❑ After you finish reading this, close your eyes. Think of a decision of whether or not you should do something. Think of all the reasons why you should or shouldn't and then let them recede to the background.
- ❑ Now, what are you sensing in your spirit, a yes, no or wait?
- ❑ Record the results in your notebook.
- ❑ Try this with a few more situations. Record the results in your notebook.

The inward voice is something we hear. It can be conversation or sounds. We will be doing two exercises with this one also. As always, get your paper and pencil handy. Take a few deep breaths. Notice what is going on around you and in you, and then let it recede into the background.

Hearing Exercise

❑ Remember a time when you were not supposed to do something and you heard a voice in your head telling you not to do it. What did it sound like? Was it loud or quiet?

❑ Remember a time when you were supposed to wait on something. Was the voice you heard telling you to wait loud or quiet?

❑ Remember a time when you were supposed to do something. Was the voice you heard telling you to do it loud or quiet?

❑ Record your answers in your notebook.

Stop, Go, Wait Exercise

❑ Remember a situation when things did not go right. Was there a sound to warn you? What did it sound like? Allow yourself to hear it. If there were a word to warn you, what would it be? Allow yourself to hear it.

❑ Remember a situation which required you to wait and be patient. What sound would you hear? Allow yourself to hear it. If there was a word, what would it be? Allow yourself to hear it.

❑ Remember a time where you needed to keep going or get started. What sound would this be? Allow yourself to hear it. If there was a word, what is it? Allow yourself to hear it.

❑ Record your answers in your notebook.

❑ Now think of a decision that you have to make. What sound are you hearing?

❑ Record it in your notebook.

❑ Do this exercise with all the decisions you need to make for the next week.

❑ Record the answers in your notebook.

Some of us see our answers rather than sensing them or hearing them. The following exercises are to see if you are a seer.

Traffic Lights Exercise 1

❑ When you see a red traffic light, what is your instinctive reaction?

❑ When you see a green traffic light, what is your instinctive reaction?

❑ When you see a yellow traffic light, what is your instinctive reaction?

Traffic Lights Exercise 2

- ❑ Imagine a traffic light. Make sure you can sense it clearly. If you can't, pretend that you can until you see it.
- ❑ Think of a current situation you are facing.
- ❑ Check the lights.
- ❑ Which light is on?
- ❑ Reflect on what the light is telling you.
- ❑ Record the results in your notebook.
- ❑ Do this with two or more situations you are facing. Record the answers in your notebook.
- ❑ Spend at least a week on this exercise and test every situation with them.
- ❑ Record the results in your notebook.

CHAPTER SIX

GOD COMMUNICATES
THROUGH EVERYDAY LIFE

As I told you before, I will be teaching you how to "hear" God the way I learned to hear Him. I learned that God communicates with us through people we encounter every day, as well as things that happen to us every day. He is an active part of our lives if we let Him be, guiding and directing us through the day. God will take natural everyday events, activities and conversations with people and give them a supernatural explanation in our lives.

Developing our spirituality and our ability to communicate with God does not mean we check our brains at the door of life. God gave us a brain and He meant for us to use it. God made us triune beings and we use all that we are to develop and grow in our spiritual lives.

Common sense is a good thing that God has given us. Jesus used it, Paul used it and we need to use it too. There was a time that Jesus knew that He and the disciples were working beyond their natural endurance so He called them away to rest. Paul thought it would be good to be left alone in Athens, so he sent others to another place to minister. There were other times he felt he needed others to be with him to help him. These were not divine revelations. These men used their brains and followed what they thought best to do. Not everything has to be "God said".

Let me give you an example of someone I know that didn't use common sense. This person was overweight, not because of any medical problem but because they overate. They would sit down to a meal and pray and ask God to remove the calories from the food. Then they would get mad at God because they were still gaining weight. That isn't God's fault. It is theirs. God is not going to remove calories from food. It goes against how He set things up. Foods contain calories because they are energy units our bodies need. He isn't going to change that. We need to learn how He set things up and work with it, not expect Him to change it, so we can do what we want to without consequences.

Then there is the counsel of others. God communicates with us through other people. In Thessalonians, Paul was speaking and he encouraged the audience to live a quiet life, to mind their own business and to work with their own hands. Then in Timothy, Paul admonished the young pastor to not let anyone keep him from doing what he was supposed to do because of his youth. He told him to give attention to reading, to exhortation, to doctrine, and not to neglect the gift that was given to him by prophecy and the laying on of hands. And he encouraged him to meditate on those things and give himself entirely to them. Listen to the good counsel of those God has put in your life. It could be a friend, a family member, a teacher or a pastor. Actually the good counsel doesn't even have to come from someone you know personally. It can come from books and from teachings on tape.

Remember that God moves in the natural. He has many ways of speaking to us and we must always be looking and staying aware, like a parent does for keeping an ear and eye open for a child. We must develop a way to stay present to the moment. I really didn't understand the importance of staying present in the moment until I heard some teachings on this from Lance Wallnau.

I'm going to give you an exercise now to do that will help you develop that awareness. Get out a pencil and paper to record your answers, and when you are finished put them in your notebook.

Awareness Exercise

When you get finished reading this, pick up your pencil and paper and record the following:

- ❑ What do you see?
- ❑ What do you hear?

- ❑ What do you feel?
- ❑ What do you taste?
- ❑ What is going through your mind?

Example From My Journal

"I hear cars going by, splashing on the wet roads from the melting snow. I hear the hum of the computer. The pen on paper. Snow sliding off the roof."

"I smell the coffee I brewed earlier and a bit of the odor of the shampoo I used to wash my hair.

"I see the snow falling gently outside. The ground and trees blanketed with snow. The sky is full of gray puffy clouds."

"There is a sense of peace looking out the window, seeing the snow falling and the cars going by. It is warm and comfy in the house."

"I taste the coffee and apple food bar that lingers pleasantly on my tongue."

"Pleasant memories of past fun filled childhood winters float through my mind. It's going to be a pleasant day."

When I did this exercise the first time, I thought it was stupid. I thought it was a waste of my valuable time when I could really be learning how to hear God for myself. I have since realized that it has become one of the most valuable tools I have. I can't remember where I first found this exercise, but I have found it many places over the years, so it's a pretty common one and is called many different things. This is an exercise I've had you doing before other exercises, and I will continue to have you do so before doing many of the others. It is important to be aware of what is going on in us normally, so that when God is showing us something we can discern it.

God Communicates Through Things

Remember that we talked about God talking to us in everyday situations? We're going to do an exercise now that will show you that. Doing this exercise on a regular basis, will help develop your awareness of when God is communicating with you throughout the day. Once again, make sure you have a pencil and paper handy. Put your answers in your notebook.

Things Exercise

After reading this, I want you to look up and the first thing your eyes notice, describe it. Now, ask the Holy Spirit to speak to you from the description. What have you been told?

Example From My Journal

It was one of my sisters' birthdays. She had been going through a rough time and I wanted to do something special for her. I went and purchased a lot of different bath items, so she could pamper herself. As I was putting them into a gift bag for her, I picked up the bath pillow and heard the following words:

"Just as the pillow is a rest for your head, so too is My Spirit a rest for your soul. Enter into My rest. Think on Me and meditate in My word and rest your weary soul."

"As the pillow cradles your head, I too want to cradle you in My peace and in My presence. Come to Me for your place of rest."

That word from the Lord for my sister not only was special for me, but it special for her as well. He knew who she was, what she was going through, and wanted to give her His rest and comfort.

Example From My Journal

"On this journal are pictures of: screws, paper clips, clothespins, faucet nozzle and handle, a child's block, sunglasses, keys, fish, passport, toothbrush, stars, paint and paintbrush, the number 4, an airplane, a fish that is blue, white and red, monopoly money, tape measure, ducks, tree, material, ribbon, a car, a bike lock, lightbulb, hair bow, scissors, popcorn, high heeled shoes, push tack, gift box, alligator and tape. Inside is paper with lines for writing."

"I chose this journal because it spoke to me as a work in progress and that's how I feel. This is what I believe God is saying to me with it: Work or play, Jesus is the key to unlock the answers we need in our lives. So often, our past haunts us and we allow Satan to really put the screws to us. Not being aware of who we really are, we have pieced together the fabric of our lives the best we knew how."

"We have a picture that we have painted in our minds of how our lives should be, who we should be, and how we should act. Most of the time, we fall short of that picture so we clean up, dress up and put a smile on our face, hoping no one will realize we're not who or what we should be."

"It is only when Jesus comes, shining His light on us that we can begin to see. He illuminates our spirit and our minds. He fills us with His Holy Spirit."

"The Holy Spirit turns on the flow of His Spirit within us, cleansing us, healing our wounds and making us whole."

"Jesus is the passport, our passport into the kingdom of God. He gives us the keys to the kingdom of God. He gives us the building blocks we need to build on day by day. Jesus is the gift we get to open, every day."

Try doing this exercise with one or two more items. Record the results in your notebook.

God Communicates Through An Audible Voice

Now I know some people are going to wonder why on earth I would put this under the everyday life situations heading, but hold on and I'll tell you. Many times the audible voice we hear, we pass off as just our imagination, because it is the voice of someone we know and we think we are just hearing things. Remember the story of Samuel in the Scriptures? He was living in Eli's house and he heard what he thought was Eli calling him in the night. The first two times he heard the voice, he went running to Eli to see what he wanted. The third time, he did as Eli instructed him and said, "Speak Lord" and finally listened to what God wanted to tell him. So remember, God may use a voice we are familiar with, a voice of someone we trust completely or who is a voice of authority to us in order to communicate with us.

Exercise

- ❑ Can you think of a time when you "heard" someone calling your name or speaking to you and no one was there?
- ❑ Could it have been God trying to get your attention?
- ❑ Did you recognize the voice as God trying to get your attention?
- ❑ Record your answers in your notebook.

God Communicates Through Situations With People

God communicates with us through everyday experiences. God taught me about how much He loves us through my granddaughter. One day, my grandchildren came over to visit I gave them some red colored punch. We have a light colored carpet. My granddaughter Kaitlynn spilled her punch. She immediately became upset saying, "I'm sorry, I'm sorry, I'm sorry." The poor girl was so upset over her accident that she was shaking and I think she expected me to be upset. Instead I replied, "Kaitlynn honey, the carpet is just a thing and people are more important than things. Let's just clean it up. Grandma's carpet is stain resistant, so don't worry about it. Even if it stains, you're more important to me than a carpet." Then the next day, we were doing something together again and she spilled something. Her reaction this time was different. She just looked at me and said, "I'm more important than things, aren't I Grandma?" I said, "Yes, sweetheart you are." And as we cleaned up the mess, I realized that this is how God wants us to feel when we've come to Him, because we've made a mess. He wants us to know He loves us and that we are important, and all the messes we make can be brought to Him without fear. Now we're going to do an exercise using this kind of example.

Exercise

Think of a time when God taught you something through an everyday experience with another person. Record it in your notebook.

God Communicates Through Books, Sermons And Teachings

I have shared with you some of the ways I have been spoken to by God through the Scriptures and prayer and meditation. That same method can be used when reading books, listening to sermons and listening to teachers. When something is highlighted to you, write it down.

Exercise

Read a book or listen to a teaching tape until God highlights something to you. Write it down and put it in your notebook.

God Communicates Through Television, Movies And The Visual Arts

Have you ever watched a program or movie and had God talk to you through it? The following are some things that God taught me through a movie.

Example From My Journal

"God taught me how important it is to stay aware at all times through the movie, 'The Last of the Mohicans'. In the movie, the English, surrendered to the French. Nathaniel, the adopted son of the Mohicans, was a prisoner of the English and as they walked along the path, I noticed that even though he was bound at the hands, he still kept himself aware of what was going on around him. It was more than that he was looking around with his eyes. Everything about him was alert and listening. He was ready, no matter what the situation. He would not be taken by surprise. God drew my attention to that and from then on, I decided that I would learn to live in awareness, not just naturally, but spiritually as well."

Example From My Journal

"The movie, 'The Matrix' is about reality and perception. After you've been born again, life has endless possibilities. In our 'past life', our perception wasn't reality. We are not really limited human beings after all. When we are born again we become aware of who and what we really are. Like in the movie, we pop in and out of the 'spirit'—true reality. Until we are debugged and unhooked from the worlds system, we cannot perceive who we really are or the kingdom we've been placed here to be a part of. When we're reborn, we are awakened to the fact that there are two kingdoms. We've been living in a kingdom that has no right to exist as a power in our lives. We are now awakened to the fact that we are meant to live in the kingdom without limits."

"The kingdom of God is within us; His spirit is within us. 'It is the world that has been pulled over your eyes to blind you to the true reality.' Until you've made the choice to be reconciled to God, you cannot get "online" to be a part of the kingdom of God and discover who He has created you to be and what He has created you to do. The only way we can know what is real is to come into the kingdom of God as His child."

Exercise

- ❑ Watch a television program, movie, or stare at a picture for a while and ask God to speak through it.
- ❑ Record your impressions in your notebook.

Exercise

- ❑ Listen to some music.
- ❑ Ask God to speak to you through it.
- ❑ Record your impressions in your notebook.

Exercise

- ❑ Look at something in nature.
- ❑ Ask God to speak to you through it.
- ❑ Record your impressions in your notebook.

Exercise

- ❑ Sit quietly for a minute.
- ❑ What thoughts are going through your mind?
- ❑ What memories do those thoughts bring back? Is God speaking to you through your thoughts?
- ❑ Record your impressions in your notebook.

Go through your notebook and look at what you've gotten so far. Use the sheet from the chapter on discerning to see what is God and what isn't. Record your answers in your notebook.

PUTTING IT ALL TOGETHER

1. Look at all your notes from the exercises you did this week. The different exercises of reading, praying and meditating on Scripture.

2. What do all your answers or experiences have in common?

   ❑ What overall themes emerge? Don't look simply for the obvious. Some can be quite inconspicuous. _____

   _____

   _____

   ❑ If they don't seem to go together, does this illuminate other things that you have wanted answers to? _____

   _____

   _____

   ❑ In what ways are they similar? _____

   _____

   _____

3. What do they tell you about what God is saying to you? What areas of your life is He speaking to? _____

   _____

   _____

4. Did this answer any questions you've had on your mind?

   _____

   _____

   _____

   _____

5. Did this bring up any new questions you'd like answers to?

   _____

   _____

   _____

   _____

   _____

TESTING WHAT YOU'RE GETTING

(Images, Thoughts, Impressions)

When asking God for His leading, these are areas we need to be especially cautious. Check to see if the word or guidance you receive is any of the following:

- ❑ Something you intensely desire.
- ❑ Something you really don't want to happen.
- ❑ Anything that is a substitute for an intimate relationship with God.
- ❑ Something that lifts up you, not God.

Adapted from "How To Hear God's Voice" by Mark and Patti Virkler
Available at www.cwgministries.org
(used with permission)

Find Its Origin, Test Its Content & Check Its Fruit 1 John 4:1,5; Matthew 7:16

SELF	GOD	ANOTHER SPIRIT
Comes from the mind/a progressive building of ideas. My wants, desires, & thoughts.	Pictures and thoughts come from the inner— most being. Sensed in spirit, then formed.	Comes from the mind. A picture or thought.
May be good or bad. Consideration of things I have learned. May or may not want to test it.	Instructive, uplifting, comforting & peaceful. Not afraid of testing.	Negative, destructive, pushy, fearful, anxious, unsettled, exhaustion, condemnation. Afraid of being tested.
Results vary.	Quickens faith, peace, good fruit, knowledge, enlightenment, strength & humility.	Fear, compulsion, bondage, anxiety, confusion, inflated ego.

CHAPTER SEVEN

GOD COMMUNICATES THROUGH
DREAMS AND VISIONS

Dreams

God communicates with us through our dreams. Now admittedly, this is not my area of expertise. I rarely remember my dreams, but when I do, they usually are dreams from God, not the ones where my mind is processing the day's activities. However, because of the research I did on this subject, I believe I can be of some help to you here. I'm not going to go into lengthy descriptions about dreams, but I will give you some advice on recalling and interpreting dreams.

If you are a dreamer, I recommend you start a dream notebook. Take seriously that God is speaking to you in your dreams. Because He is speaking, it is important for you to listen. Interpreting dreams takes effort, self-discipline and requires time and energy, but it is worth the effort.

Recalling Dreams

- ❏ Ask God to speak to you through dreams.
- ❏ Expect to receive dreams.
- ❏ When you wake up, be still for a moment and see if you can recall a dream.
- ❏ Write down your dreams and all the details.
- ❏ Don't give up if you don't remember one. It takes expectancy.

❑ Record each dream and date it.

Interpreting Dreams

❑ Remember dreams speak symbolically, so seek associations for each symbol of the dream.
❑ Divide the dream into sections that seem to go together.
❑ Divide each section into small pieces.
❑ Ask God to tell you what each piece means.
❑ Ask yourself questions about each piece of the dream.
❑ Relate the dream to your circumstances.
❑ Why is that piece in the dream?
❑ What could it stand for?
❑ If I think of the piece as a symbol, what would it be associated with?
❑ Where did the dream occur?
❑ Why did I behave that way?

Example From My Journal

"The dream:

> *In my dream, there was a manual can opener as large as a man. It was standing next to a man. No one I knew, just a man. Date: September 2001*"

"The process:

❑ Manual can opener—not automatic
❑ Large enough to open a man"

"Interpretation October 7, 2001
We have been given a tool, (gifts of the Holy Spirit), large enough to open up whatever has been sealed and preserved in people. In us has been preserved all the tools, (gifts of the Holy Spirit), necessary to help others. We just need to use the tools to open up and help others, whatever their needs are. We have to choose to. It is not automatic."

Exercise:

Begin keeping a notebook exclusively for your dreams and visions. Include in it pages for:

- ❑ Colors and what they mean to you.
- ❑ Polarities, (hot/cold, hard/soft etc.) and what they mean to you.
- ❑ Numbers and what they mean to you.
- ❑ Symbols and what they mean to you.

Visions

This is one of the ways God speaks that absolutely seems to cause the church to cringe. We can accept dreams; after all you're asleep and can't help it. But if you have visions, well, it must mean either you're really spiritual or you're imagining things or you're weird. I think it is atrocious the way some in the church belittle people who have visions. These people are neither weird, nor are they superspiritual. It is the way God has chosen to communicate with them. Some churches believe visions are okay, but it is not okay to ask for them. I disagree. As a matter of fact, I believe we are supposed to receive communication from God in many different ways. Ever looked at people? God is into variety! Mark and Patti Virkler have written an excellent book about expecting to see visions called, "How to Hear God's Voice". I think it is a must read for anyone who wants to hear God's voice and see visions on a regular basis. In their book, they use one Scripture in describing how we should approach God to see visions. It is found in Habakkuk 2:1-2. They have broken the Scripture down into four keys (page 5 in their book).

- ❑ "I will stand on my guardpost . . ."—Have a quiet place to quiet yourself before the Lord.
- ❑ "And I will keep watch to see . . ."—Look for vision as you pray.
- ❑ "And He will speak to me . . ."—Recognize God's voice as a flow of spontaneous thoughts (let me add here, vision).
- ❑ "Then the Lord answered me and said, 'Record the vision . . .'"—Record God's words (let me add here and the vision) in your notebook.

Now remember that Jesus Himself said He only did the things He saw His Father do. Jesus is our example and we should be living out of the spontaneous flow of what we see our Father wanting to do. For those who have a problem with expecting to see visions in this manner, I have an assignment for you to look up the following Scriptures. But don't just look them up. Write them out and put them in your notebook. This is not an exhaustive list. You can look up more if you'd like. We will also include some verses about dreams in this list.

Assignment—Look up and write out the following verses:

DREAMS

Genesis:	Job:	Daniel:
20:3, 6	7:14	1:17
28:12	20:8	2:1-26
31:24	30:15,16	4:5
31:10-12		5:12
37:5-20	I Samuel 28:13-15	7:1-16
40:5-16		
41:1-32	II Samuel 7:4-17	Joel 2:28
42:9		
	I Kings 3:5-15	Matthew:
Numbers 12:6		1:20
		2:12-22
Judges 7:13-15		
		Acts 2:17

VISIONS

Genesis 15:1	Isaiah:	Luke 1:22
	1:1	
	6:1-10	

Numbers 12:6   Ezekiel: Acts:
                        1:1-4   2:17
                        7:13-26   10:3-19
                        8:3-7   11:5-6
                        11:1,24   12:9
                        40:2-6   16:9-10
                        43:1-6   18:9
                        44:1-5

Judges: Joel 2:28   II Corinthian 12:11
6:12-14
13:3-20

I Samuel 3:1-15   Job: Revelations 9:14
                        7:14
                        20:8

I Chronicles 17:15   Obadiah 1:1

II Chronicles 32:32   Nahum 1:1

Psalms 89:19   Proverbs 29:18

VISIONS OF THE NIGHT

Genesis 46:2-4   Job: 4:13-16   Daniel:
                                               8:1-27
                                               9:21-24

LOOK

Exodus: 3:1-6 16:9-11	Ezekiel: 2:9 10:1-9	Mark 9:8
Joshua 5:13-15	Daniel 12:5	Acts: 1:10 7:55
Psalms 5:3	Zechariah: 2:1 4:2 5:1, 5, 9 6:1	II Corinthians 4:18
Isaiah: 8:17 17:7-8 40:25-26 42:18		Revelation: 4:1-3 6:8 14:1,14 15:5

EYES

Genesis: 3:5-7 21:19 31:10	Psalms: 25:15 119:18 123:2 141:8	Matthew 13:15-16
Exodus 24:15-18	Isaiah 44:18	Acts: 26:18-19 28:27
Numbers: 22:31 24:2-4	Jeremiah 5:21	Romans 11:8,10
II Kings 6:17	Ezekiel 12:2 Zechariah 1:18	Ephesians 1:18

You may also want to look up Scriptures on words such as "behold", "see" and "watch". Record the results in your notebook.

Now that you've finished that assignment, I hope you're convinced from the Scriptures that God does want to show you things visually, and that the spontaneous flow of vision comes from Him. If you're still not convinced, continue studying and asking God to show you.

I have some more exercises for you to do in order to jump-start you into seeing a spontaneous flow of vision. Before you do the assignments, I want to reassure you that God is in control. Ask for His help and He will help you. Remember that you will be judging everything you get, so go ahead and record it all until it is time to judge it. This is practice, so practice away without fear.

Do This Exercise Before Any Of The Following Exercises:

- ❑ Get quiet within yourself.
- ❑ Notice what you're thinking and feeling; the thoughts that are going through your mind.
- ❑ Now let them recede into the background.
- ❑ Ask the Holy Spirit to allow you to see a spontaneous flow of vision for what He wants to show you.
- ❑ Do one or more of the exercises below.

Scripture Exercise:

- ❑ Go to I John 2:20. Read it and ask the Lord to show you how it is possible to "know all things."
- ❑ Then, close your eyes and imagine yourself connecting on the inside, your spirit to the Spirit of the living God.
- ❑ Let yourself see Him talking with you face to face. Let yourself see Him showing you the things you need to know.
- ❑ Record your results in your notebook. Include anything you were thinking or feeling. Don't leave anything out.

Scripture Exercise:

❑ Go to John 5:19. Sit and think on the Scripture where it says that the Son can do nothing of Himself, but what He sees the Father do. Ask God to show you how to make this real in your life.

❑ After you finish reading this exercise, close your eyes.

❑ Imagine yourself watching the Father intently as He shows you what to do.

❑ See yourself getting up and doing what He has shown you.

❑ Sit and think on it for a while.

❑ Now record in your notebook what you saw.

Scripture Exercise:

❑ Pick a Bible story from the gospels, any one of your choosing. It can be of Jesus picking His disciples, raising the dead, any that you like.

❑ See yourself in that story with Him. Imagine seeing Jesus face to face. Imagine how you will interact with Him, how you will respond to the things He is doing and saying.

❑ Record your experience in your notebook. What you saw, what you felt, what you heard, what your smelled, and what you tasted.

❑ Now go look at the end of this chapter and use the sheet on how to test what you are getting. It will help you judge what you've been experiencing. Don't worry if it didn't come from God, yet.

Continue to practice, expecting God to communicate with you in this way. We'll be doing a lot more on this later in the book.

Envelope Exercise:

Remember the envelopes from the chapter on hearing God through the Scriptures? Take a week for each envelope and ask God to speak to you any way He wants to for that question. Stay alert and record your answers each day. Remember that it could be through memories, movies, books, preaching, Scripture, dreams, visions, or any everyday activity.

❑ Week one, envelope one.

❑ Week two, envelope two.

❑ Week three, envelope three.
❑ At the end of the three weeks, look over the answers you've received for each of the envelopes. Gather together all the answers for each one. Open the envelopes. How do the answers fit the questions? Record your results. How did you do hearing from God without knowing what the question was? Record your answers. Was it God you were hearing? Look at the sheet on learning to discern. Have your spiritual counselor or accountability partner look over your answers. Accept what is God and throw out what isn't. You are learning. Expect to make mistakes.

WEEKLY SPIRITUAL EXERCISE
PUTTING IT ALL TOGETHER

1. Look at all your notes from the exercises you did this week. The different exercises of reading, praying and meditating on Scripture.
2. What do all the Scriptures have in common?

    ❑ What overall themes emerge? Don't look simply for the obvious. Some can be quite inconspicuous. _____
    _____
    _____

    ❑ If they don't seem to go together, does this illuminate other things that you have wanted answers to? _____
    _____
    _____

    ❑ In what ways are they similar? _____
    _____
    _____

3. What do they tell you about what God is saying to you? What areas of your life is He speaking to? _____
    _____
    _____

4. Did this answer any questions you've had on your mind?
    _____
    _____
    _____

5. Did this bring up any new questions you'd like answers to?
    _____
    _____
    _____
    _____

TESTING WHAT YOU'RE GETTING

(Images, Thoughts, Impressions)

When asking God for His leading, these are areas we need to be especially cautious. Check to see if the word or guidance you receive is any of the following:

- ☐ Something you intensely desire.
- ☐ Something you really don't want to happen.
- ☐ Anything that is a substitute for an intimate relationship with God.
- ☐ Something that lifts up you, not God.

Adapted from "How To Hear God's Voice" by Mark & Patti Virkler
Available at www.cwgministries.org
(used with permission)

Find Its Origin, Test Its Content & Check Its Fruit 1 John 4:1,5;
Matthew 7:16

SELF	GOD	ANOTHER SPIRIT
Comes from the mind/a progressive building of ideas. My wants, desires, & thoughts.	Pictures and thoughts come from the inner—most being. Sensed in spirit, then formed.	Comes to the mind. A picture or thought.
May be good or bad. Consideration of things I have learned. May or may not want to test it.	Instructive, uplifting, comforting & peaceful. Not afraid of testing.	Negative, destructive, pushy, fearful, anxious, unsettled, exhaustion, condemnation. Afraid of being tested.
Results vary.	Quickens faith, peace, good fruit, knowledge, enlightenment, strength & humility.	Fear, compulsion, bondage, anxiety, confusion, inflated ego.

CHAPTER EIGHT

GOD COMMUNICATES THROUGH
THE GIFTS OF THE SPIRIT

The gifts of the Holy Spirit are given to us by the Spirit Himself. We are the vessels, the channel these gifts flow through; to say the things He wants to say, giving us revelation knowledge that will help us or someone else; to do the things He wants to do on this earth for those He wants to touch. What's wonderful about the way God moves through us to touch someone is that He moves through our personality, our nature and our character. No two people present God the same way! He really does love variety! Think He doesn't want to speak or touch through you? He doesn't move through us because we are super spiritual or because we are holier than someone else is. He moves through us because of His grace and because we will allow Him to. The Holy Spirit gives gifts to us as He wills. In the Old Testament, He spoke through an ass to give a message. I think He can speak through us! While we can be vessels He works through once in a while, we can make ourselves available on a regular basis. We can allow ourselves to mature, to grow in the anointing He has given us. We can allow ourselves to be trained, so that we have depth and accuracy impacting the church and the world for God's glory.

The gifts are divided into three categories with three gifts in each category. The categories are the gifts of utterance, the gifts of revelation, and the gifts of power.

The key to operating in the gifts is to make ourselves available, asking Him whom He'd like to touch or speak to, and then expect Him to do it through us. It's important to have faith that He will move through you because of His mercy and His grace. Learn to expect the gifts to be in operation through you. Allow yourself to be a channel by doing what you see or hear or sense spontaneously. Pay attention to that prompting or urge that comes like a desire. Remember that He puts His desires in our hearts. Don't be afraid to make mistakes. If you miss it, just say so. Remember that in Romans 12:6, it tells us to operate in the gifts in proportion to our faith. We build up faith by hearing the word and then acting on it.

We will be discussing two of the gifts categories: the gifts of revelation and the utterance gifts. After we discuss them, we will be doing exercises to prepare ourselves to operate in the gifts.

The Revelation Gifts

The revelation gifts are gifts where you know something through the Holy Spirit revealing to you a word of knowledge, a word of wisdom or through the discerning of spirits. Revelation gifts show what is hidden of the past, present and future. They reveal the realm of the spirit world that we cannot see with our natural eyes. Revelation gifts bring the mind of God to the people. They give us God's perspective of a circumstance, a person, or a problem. The Holy Spirit reveals the mind of Christ and God's thoughts to us, bringing answers and keys to overcoming whatever is keeping us from being all He has created us to be. Revelation gifts give us whatever we need to know to minister accurately and effectively to those He wants to touch. He reveals how God is working in our lives through the past experiences, working them out for our good. He uses the revelation gifts to speak to our hearts how He feels about us making our self image to become the image He has for us as His children. He speaks to our future, the plans and purposes He has for our lives. The revelation gifts are as important for us in the church today as they were two thousand years ago. We still need the mind and heart of God revealed to the world today. Let's look at the revelation gifts individually.

The Word of Knowledge

The first revelation gift we will be talking about is the word of knowledge. This gift is a divine revelation from God that tells or shows us what is happening right now, or what has happened in the past. It is a word of God's knowledge for a particular season or time, for a person or group of people or for a particular purpose or place. It can be a word of knowledge that enlightens the truths of the written Word, or one that reveals specific knowledge or information about a person's, (or group of people such as a nation or church), past or present. It is a fragment of the knowledge of God, but is the specific word that is needed for the situation or person involved. It is not a naturally acquired knowledge or knowledge acquired from a long experience with God. It is knowledge given for a specific time or person and purpose. An example of that could be when God wants to bring healing to a person, or a group of people.

The word of knowledge can come to us supernaturally in different ways. We may receive words in our mind, receive a sense of what God is revealing, we may get a physical sensation, (an ache or pain that reveals where a person needs healing), we may receive a vision and interpretation, a message through a song or through the remembrance of Scripture. In other words, through seeing, sensing or hearing. That is why it is important to know how God talks to us. When God shows or tells us something about a person our response to that should be to ask Him what He wants us to do with it. Sometimes it's just to pray. At other times, it is information we need in order to allow us to speak something into their life. When the Holy Spirit reveals something about someone, it is to help them and not to hurt them. It is important that we learn how to handle what He shares with us.

Let me give you an example of a word of knowledge. I was talking with someone one day about what was going on in their life. As we were talking, I "sensed" that she had been abused as a child. So while we were talking, I asked God what He wanted me to do with this knowledge. She hadn't ever told anyone, so when I told her that God wanted to heal the wounds she had because of the abuse, she allowed me to pray for her right then. What that did for her was it made her aware that God knows who she is, He cares for her and He wants to remove her pain. It caused her to desire to know God for herself. When I asked God what to do about the situation, He gave me a word of wisdom.

Ask God to allow you to receive the gift of the word of knowledge to help someone He would like to speak to. Remain open to receiving the word of knowledge from Him. Practice hearing God's voice, and stay sensitive to the Holy Spirit.

Exercise

Keep a paper and pencil handy.

- ❑ Begin to pray for a loved one.
- ❑ Ask God to give you a word of knowledge for them.
- ❑ Ask God what the person needs to hear from Him.
- ❑ What area of their life needs His touch?
- ❑ After you have prayed, record any thoughts you have, whatever is going through your mind, any feelings you are having.
- ❑ Ask God if this is something you need to share with the person or if you need to pray the situation through for them.
- ❑ Record the results in your notebook.

The Word of Wisdom

The word of wisdom is a divine revelation from God that gives supernatural insight on how to deal with things that have happened or that are going to happen in the future. It is the ability in the Spirit to impart special information, insight, guidance or counsel that illuminates the situation, revealing God's will and purposes to be carried out and established. While it is often futuristic, it is different from prophecy, because it tells you how to deal with something, while prophecy tells you what will happen. It is the Holy Spirit's supernatural revelation of the mind of Christ concerning the future plans and purposes of God for a person, situation, church or nation. It's the unfolding of God's will and purposes that He desires to be carried out and established in the lives of those concerned. It isn't common sense, or wisdom acquired by living a godly life. It also is not a code of ethics, or learned earthly wisdom. It isn't a deep spiritual insight or an understanding of the ways of God. It is a word of wisdom the Holy Spirit gives as it is needed. The word of wisdom will tell you how to handle a situation in your life that you're not sure how to handle. Take the example of the word of knowledge previously given. God not only told her that He knew what had happened to her, (word of knowledge), He also told her He wanted to heal her, (word of knowledge again), and that her healing would help others as she shared what God had done for her, (word of wisdom).

Ask God to allow you to receive a word of wisdom from Him for someone He would like to speak to. Remain open for Him to do so.

Exercise

Keep a pencil and paper handy.

- ❑ Begin to pray for an individual that comes to mind.
- ❑ Ask God to give you a word of wisdom for them.
- ❑ Begin to write what comes to your mind, the impressions you receive and the feeling you have.
- ❑ Is it something you need to pray through or is it something you need to share with that person?
- ❑ Record the results in your notebook.

Practice Sessions

Giving a spiritual word, (word of knowledge, word of wisdom or prophecy), is not taking a test—so don't worry about whether your impressions are "right" or "wrong." Your spirit is gathering information, which you will process and decide whether it is from the Holy Spirit, or not.

Trust your spirit. Allow yourself to notice the images or symbols and other impressions, (smells, sounds, feelings), you might receive.

The impressions you receive do not have to make sense to you. They may be things that make sense to the person you are praying for, so be careful to record your information, not judge it.

Simply allow yourself to record or speak what you're picking up.

The idea is to make mistakes. This is how we learn. Give yourself permission to make them.

Record everything—even things that seem like interference to you.

If you feel like you aren't getting anything, make something up. What might seem like guesses and imagination can be very accurate information from the Holy Spirit.

"I know I'm not getting anything, but if I could, this is what it would be." Go from there.

Record your thought, picture or word from God. It may come in the form of a mental impression; a thought or word, a Scripture or song, a picture or you may get a physical sensation. Record whatever you get in your notebook.

The Discerning of Spirits

The discerning of spirits is a divine ability to see or sense or hear spirits. It is the supernatural ability to identify the nature and character of those spirits, seen or unseen. It gives us supernatural insights into the realm of the spirits. We will know when it is the Holy Spirit, an angel, ungodly spirits, (demons), the spirit of man, or a person's motivation for the things they do or say, including our own. We will know the difference. That is a gift that the Holy Spirit gives to His people. It is not the ability to see faults in another. It is not a spirit of suspicion, and it is not psychological insight, nor is it the natural discernment that we are all supposed to develop. This is the ability to discern spirits; the Holy Spirit, angels, ungodly spirits, or the spirit of a man in operation.

Ask God to allow you the gift of discerning of spirits, so that you can know what is of Him and what is not of Him. Watch for it to begin to operate in your life.

Exercise

Develop your natural discernment, while believing God for the gift of discerning of spirits.

The Utterance Gifts

These are uttered or spoken gifts, often feeling as if the Holy Spirit is speaking through you directly for whatever purpose. These include the gifts of prophecy, diverse tongues, and interpretation of tongues.

The Gift of Prophecy

Prophecy is a supernatural utterance in your own language. It is given to bring the word of the Lord to a nation, congregation, or an individual. Prophecy means to flow forth, to bubble forth, to tumble forth, or to spring forth. Prophecy is conditional. It confirms and it should edify, exhort, and/or comfort. Prophecy is the Spirit of God speaking to the spirit of man. It's coming from your spirit. As I stated before, prophecy informs you what will happen in the future, what He has planned for you. The simple gift of prophecy is non-directive, encouraging, inspirational, and seeks to bless the body of Christ while glorifying the Lord. Using the example I used in the word of knowledge and the word of wisdom, God went on and spoke to this person, that He would use the pain she had been through to help heal others. As she shared her story with others, it would help them, and that she is a healer of the wounded. That prophetic word is telling her who she is and what her future is going to bring. That is a word of prophecy. You can clearly see how prophecy brings together the word of knowledge and the word of wisdom. Just because you give a prophetic word does not mean you are a prophet. Everyone can and should be developing their prophetic gifting. God wants to speak through all of us to someone in the simple gift of prophecy, to encourage and comfort one another. Scripture tells us in 1 Corinthians 14 that we should covet to prophesy, so it is not wrong to want to prophesy, and we should prepare ourselves to be able to hear from God so that we can.

Because the gift of prophecy is a spoken gift, I am going to give you some exercises to help you learn to speak what you are getting out loud. These you will record in your notebook later, but for these exercises now you will need a tape recorder and some blank cassette tapes.

The following exercise is one that will help you learn how to keep in the flow of God and not hinder the Holy Spirit. It is intended to help you learn what God may be saying before you can filter or edit it anything out, so keep a continuous flow of speaking.

Exercise

- ❑ Pray. "I submit every thought of my soul and my spirit to the mind of Christ. I will receive thoughts, impressions, words, and pictures from the Holy Spirit."
- ❑ Believe you will receive.
- ❑ Tune in and listen.
- ❑ For _____ minutes (start with one and work up to fifteen), speak out everything that comes to your mind. Don't worry if it doesn't make sense, or if it's God or your own heart. Your job is to listen and speak

without filtering or editing anything. (I see, I hear, I sense, I feel, I taste, I think etc.)
- ❏ Do this every day until it becomes easy.
- ❏ Record your results in your notebook.

Practice Sessions

Choose a person to prophesy over. Picture them in your mind.

Pray before you begin, asking for God to speak to you and bring your every thought captive to His thoughts.

Giving a spiritual word, (word of knowledge, word of wisdom or prophetic word), is not taking a test—so don't worry about whether your impressions are "right" or "wrong." Your spirit is gathering information, which you will determine later to know whether it is from the Holy Spirit or not.

Trust your spirit. Allow yourself to notice the images or symbols and other impressions, (smells, sounds, feelings), you might receive.

The impressions you receive do not have to make sense to you. They may be things that make sense to the person you are prophesying over, so be careful to record your information, not judge it.

Simply allow yourself to report what you're picking up.

The idea is to make mistakes. This is how we learn. Give yourself permission to make them.

Record everything—even impressions that seem like interference.

If you feel like you aren't getting anything, make something up. What seems like a guess can be a very accurate word from the Holy Spirit. "I know I'm not getting anything, but if I could, this is what it would be." Go from there.

Record in your recorder your thought, picture or word from God.

- ❏ This is what I saw.
- ❏ This is what I felt.

❏ This is what I sensed.
❏ This is what I heard.

Enter your results in your notebook. Keep practicing.

We will be doing many more exercises in the last section of this book where we will be working on developing your prophetic gift.

Divers Kinds of Tongues

This is when you speak in a language you do not know. It could be your prayer language from when you were baptized in the Holy Spirit or it could be a known language you do not know.

Interpretation of Tongues

This is when you interpret or someone else interprets the tongues you have just spoken. When God gives an interpretation in tongues, you will feel the prompting or desire to speak it. You may not have the whole message, so just start with what you have and let God give the rest!

Tongues and interpretation exercise

You will need a handheld tape recorder and a blank tape for this. Ask God to speak to you through tongues and interpretation.

❏ Start the recorder and begin speaking in tongues.
❏ When you are finished, start speaking in your natural language what you are seeing or hearing or feeling, or what is going through your mind. You may automatically switch to your natural language as you are praying in tongues. I discovered that this was the natural interpretation.
❏ Stop when you sense that you are finished.
❏ You may want to sing to God in tongues and then ask for the interpretation.
❏ Don't get hung up on this if you haven't done it before. Just practice until it becomes natural for you.
❏ Record your results in your notebook.

CHAPTER NINE

HOW DO YOU HEAR?

As we grow in our relationship with God, we will grow in our ability to hear and discern His voice. There are several ways to hear God's voice, however they all fall into three categories. Those categories are seeing, hearing and sensing. A seer is one who "sees" through a dream or vision or from mental images. A hearer "hears," often in the form of direct conversation in their mind, but sometimes it is audible. A sensor is one who just "knows" or "feels" what God is telling them. Some teachers might call it intuition.

God has given us examples of all of these throughout the Scriptures. Let's look at a few examples:

Seer

Acts 10:9-20 NKJV

"The next day, as they went on their journey and drew near the city, Peter went up on the housetop to pray, about the sixth hour. Then he became very hungry and wanted to eat; but while they made ready, he fell into a trance and saw heaven opened and an object like a great sheet bound at the four corners, descending to him and let down to the earth. In it were all kinds of four-footed animals of the earth, wild beasts, creeping things, and birds of the air. And a voice came to him, 'Rise, Peter; kill and eat.' But Peter said. 'Not so, Lord! For I have never eaten anything common or unclean.' And a voice spoke to him again the second time, 'What God has cleansed you must not call common.' This was done three times. And the object was taken up into heaven again Now while Peter wondered within

himself what this vision which he had seen meant, behold, the men who had been sent from Cornelius had made inquiry for Simon's house, and stood before the gate. And they called and asked whether Simon, whose surname was Peter, was lodging there. While Peter thought about the vision, the Spirit said to him, 'Behold, three men are seeking you. Arise therefore, go down and go with them, doubting nothing; for I have sent them.'"

In this case, the seeing came as a vision, a trance. He both saw and heard. Other examples can be found in 2 Kings 6:17, Isaiah 6:1, Amos 7:1-3, John 1:48 and Revelation 10:1-5. Examples of seers in Scripture are Amos, Paul, Peter and Cornelius.

We see in different ways, from seeing something spontaneously in our minds (mental imaging), through things we see such as creation, movies, television, circumstances, visions, dreams or memories we see happening in our minds.

Exercise

Has the Lord ever drawn your attention to something or fixed your gaze on someone? What was He showing you? How did the understanding come that He was speaking to you? Write your answers in your notebook.

Hearer

Look at the example in Acts above. It is an example of hearing. Other Scripture references for hearers are found in 1 Kings 14:2, 5 and 19:11-13, 2 Kings 7:6, Revelations chapters 6-8 and 10:3-4. Examples of hearers in Scripture are Hosea, Moses, Samuel and Ezekiel.

Ways of hearing are through intensely focused thoughts brought to our mind, recalling conversation to our memories, bringing Scripture to our memories, and bringing songs back to our memories.

Exercise

Have you ever had something brought to memory and realized it was the Lord speaking? How did you know it was God? What was He saying to you? How did the understanding come?

Sensor

Jonah 1:8-10

"'Then they said to him, Please tell us! For whose cause is this trouble upon us? What is your occupation? And where do you come from? What is your country? And of what people are you?' so he said to them, 'I am a Hebrew; and I fear the Lord, the God of heaven, who made the sea and the dry land.' Then the men were exceedingly afraid, and said to him, 'Why have you done this?' For the men knew that he fled the presence of the Lord, because he had told them."

So, these men had sensed that Jonah was fleeing the Lord, because the Lord had told them. Some sensors in the Scriptures are Jonah, Daniel, Nehemiah, Elisha, Elijah and Samuel.

Some of the ways that we sense are through feeling a word of knowledge, (you hurt where someone is hurting while you're praying for them), a sense of taste, smell, feelings and/or memories of a feeling. Also, you "just know" or an understanding just comes to you. You may feel a strong conviction of peace or a restraint in your spirit, some may say it's a "gut feeling".

Exercise

Have you ever had an instance where you have just known something and knew it was God speaking to you? What was He saying to you? How did the understanding come to you? Record your answers in your notebook.

Exercise

From the different exercises we have done so far, have you noticed which way you are best able to perceive God's voice for yourself? Record your answer in your notebook.

As you continue through the book I would like you to pay close attention to how you best hear God. Go through the different ways of hearing again and practice asking God to speak to you through the different ways. Remain open to the Holy Spirit communicating with you on a daily basis.

Practice the following exercise for at least a few days to help you notice how you hear from God.

Awareness Exercise

I first learned this exercise from Mark Chirona, but cannot remember if I read it in one of his books or heard it on a tape.

- ❑ Take a few deep breaths to calm your heart and mind. Now, pay attention to what you're noticing.
- ❑ What do you hear? How do you hear it? Can you describe it?
- ❑ What do you see? How do you see it? Can you describe it?
- ❑ What do you feel? How do you feel it? Can you describe it?
- ❑ What do you taste? How do you taste it? Can you describe it?
- ❑ What is going through your mind? Pictures or sound? Can you describe it?
- ❑ Record your answers in your notebook.

On the next page you will find a sheet that shows you at a glance how we hear from God.

WAYS OF HEARING GOD

There are several ways to hear God's voice. However they all fall into three categories: seeing, hearing and sensing.

SEER	HEARER	SENSOR
A seer is one who sees.	Direct conversation in your mind: "I heard my mind say . . ."	A sensor is one who "just knows" or "feels" what God is telling them. It seems natural and feels right. Some call it being intuitive.

Scriptures References For Each:

Amos 7:1-3; 8:13	Exodus 3:4	Nehemiah 6:2-13
Acts 10; John 1:48	Ezekiel 4:14-16	Daniel 9:1-3
Revelations 10:1-5	Hosea 1	Jonah 1:8-12
	Revelations 10:3-4, 6-11	Revelations 10:20

Examples In Scriptures For Each:

Amos, Paul, Peter, Cornelius, Elijah, Samuel	Hosea, Moses, Samuel, Ezekiel	Jonah, Daniel Nehemiah, Elisha

Ways We See, Hear And Sense:

Physical eyes, pictures in your mind, dreams, conversations,	Physical ears, memories of taste, smell, a "gut feeling". Spontaneous thoughts or conversation in your mind.	Physical senses, spiritual senses, visions, memories.

Has the Lord ever drawn your attention to something or fixed your gaze on someone? What was He showing you? How did the understanding come?

Have you ever had something brought to memory and realized it was the Lord speaking? What was He saying to you?

Have you ever just known something and knew it was God speaking to you? What was He showing you?

SECTION THREE

The Mystic Way

CHAPTER TEN

MYSTICAL CHRISTIANITY

There seems to be some confusion as to what a mystic actually is. So many people think that to mention the words "Christian" and "mystic" together is an oxymoron. But a mystic is simply someone who loves God and seeks communion and intimacy with Him through contemplation and meditation. Mysticism is the doctrine that says it is possible to achieve communion with God through contemplation and meditation. The mystical life of a Christian is a life in which the Holy Spirit guides and directs the lover of God in knowing Him and His ways. Mysticism is not blanking your mind nor does it require you to stop all critical thinking. Mysticism is not trying to become one with God. We don't need to try to become one with God because when we've received Jesus as savior, we've already been made one with Him. What we are doing is meeting with God, spirit to Spirit. So, if you're a lover of God, if you really want to know Him and have an intimate relationship with Him, if you are seeking Him with your whole body, soul and spirit, you are a mystic.

It continually amazes me how people will say that God is the same yesterday, today and forever. They will recount how there is nothing new under the sun, but then balk at taking the Scriptures and acting on them. They will say that this part of the Scripture isn't for today, or that God isn't doing this anymore and on and on and on, making the word of God of no effect in their lives today. It's so sad. What I want to do in this chapter is talk about how the ancients met with God, both from Scripture and those who came later. What I found in studying their lives is that while their methods may have been different, what they all had in common is that they meditated in order to develop their intimacy with God. David, who God said was a man after His own heart, continually spent time considering God's creation and majesty. Korah's sons contemplated intimacy with God. Mary pondered the person of Jesus, and John thought on the cross. Later Christians wanted to follow the teachings of the apostles to pray continually and developed methods to help them do that, (to always have God in their hearts and minds). We will look at some of their methods.

Now I can just hear someone thinking, "Hey wait a minute. A lot of those mystics got off into error". That is true. That is why we have spent time learning how to judge something, how to know if something is of God, of our own selves, or of an ungodly spirit. We don't throw the baby out with the bath water; we take what is God and throw the rest out. Everything is to be judged by the Scriptures and the character of God. If some of the methods don't sit right in your spirit, don't do them. But don't judge them by what others have said. Judge them by the Scriptures. Acts 17:11 says that the Bereans were more fair-minded than others in Thessalonica, because they received the word with all readiness, and searched the Scriptures daily to find out whether these things be true. That is all I'm asking you to do. Let's look at some Scriptures on meditation, so that you can see for yourself that it really is a valid scriptural practice, just in case you're unsure. I've pulled these all from Psalms and used the New King James Version of the Bible.

49:3 "My mouth shall speak wisdom, and the mediation of my heart shall give understanding."

77:6 "I call to remembrance my song in the night; I meditate within my heart, and my spirit makes diligent search."

104:34 "May my meditation be sweet to him, I will be glad in the lord."

119:97-99 "Oh, how I love your law! It is my mediation all the day. You, through your commandments, make me wiser than my enemies; for they are ever with me. I have more understanding than all my teachers for Your testimonies are my meditation."

119:148 "My eyes are awake through the night watches, that I may meditate on Your word."

Other Scriptures On Meditation

Genesis:
19:27,28
24:63

Numbers 15:38-40

Deuteronomy:
4:9,10,29,39
7:17-19
8:2

Joshua 1:8,9

Malachi 3:16

Psalms:
1:2
4:4
5:1
19:14
37:4,31
40:8
46:8,10
48:9
49:3
57:4
63:6
77:5-6, 10-12

Romans:
7:22
12:2

2 Corinthians 3:18

Philippians:
2:5
4:8

Colossians:
3:12
3:16

Proverbs:
2:1-2, 5
4:4, 20-21, 26
7:1-3
23:12
24:32

Psalms continued:
90:12
91:1
103:2
104:34
119:11,15,18,27, 36-
37, 47-48, 77-78, 93,
97-99, 159

1 Timothy 4:14, 15

Isaiah 46:9

While this is not an exhaustive list, it is a place to start. You can look in a concordance for more verses. You may also want to look under the following words:

- ❏ Remember
- ❏ Think on these things
- ❏ Ponder
- ❏ Behold
- ❏ Muse

- ☐ Consider
- ☐ Let the mind of Christ be in you
- ☐ Set your mind on things above
- ☐ Let the word of Christ dwell in you

Meditation reminds us of God and motivates us to understand our roles in life. After meditation comes action. And remember, we are not trying to become one with God, because we are already one with Him. Meditation renews your mind, brings discipline to your body, and strengthens your spirit. It causes you to grow as a Christian and helps enable you to walk out life in the spirit. Meditation is a part of renewing of our minds so that we realize that we are spiritual beings and sons of the Most High God. We have indeed been made a partaker of His divine nature. See 1 John 3:1 and 2 Peter 1:4.

Benefits of Meditation

- ☐ Develop intimacy with God
- ☐ Gain insight and instruction
- ☐ Get a clear focus
- ☐ Peace of God

When to Meditate

- ☐ During prayer
- ☐ When reading Scripture
- ☐ While driving to work
- ☐ Showering or bathing
- ☐ Putting on makeup or shaving
- ☐ Running errands
- ☐ Waiting
- ☐ In bed—before sleep or upon waking
- ☐ Any time you want to set aside to be alone with God

Christian meditation fills our minds with God and who He is, who He has created us to be. It causes us to do what He has sent us here to do. He becomes our focus and rather than causing us to want to retreat from the world, it prepares us to deal with life effectively. Meditation grounds us in Scripture, in God and His ways. Meditation is romancing God.

Tools for Meditation

❏ Bible
❏ Paper
❏ Pen or Pencil
❏ Tape recorder and blank tapes

Postures for Meditation

❏ Sitting
❏ Standing
❏ Lying down
❏ Kneeling
❏ Walking

Romancing God during Meditation

❏ Music
❏ Candles
❏ Incense
❏ Poetry

Now let's examine some of the mystics from the Bible. One of the best known is David.

Psalm 32 (a contemplation of David, NKJV). In case you don't know, selah means stop and think on this.

Verses 1-4 (David thinks on those who are blessed because they are forgiven.)

"Blessed is he whose transgression is forgiven, whose sin is covered. Blessed is the man to whom the Lord does not impute iniquity, and in whose spirit there is no deceit. When I kept silent, my bones grew old through my groaning all the day long. For day and night Your hand was heavy upon me; my vitality was turned into the drought of summer. Selah."

Verse 5 (David thinks on how God forgave him.)

"I acknowledged my sin to You, and my iniquity I have not hidden. I said, 'I will confess my transgressions to the Lord,' and You forgave the iniquity of my sin. Selah."

Verses 6-7 (David thinks on why people should pray to God and how God protects his own.)

"For this cause everyone who is godly shall pray to You in a time when You may be found; surely in a flood of great waters they shall not come near him. You are my hiding place; You shall preserve me from trouble; You shall surround me with songs of deliverance. Selah."

Verses 8-11 (God talks back to David.)

"I will instruct you and teach you in the way you should go; I will guide you with My eye. Do not be like the horse or like the mule, which have no understanding, which must be harnessed with bit and bridle, else they will not come near you. Many sorrows shall be to the wicked; but he who trusts in the Lord, mercy shall surround him. Be glad in the Lord and rejoice, you righteous; and shout for joy, all you upright in heart!"

So we can see from David's example when we sit and contemplate on God, He talks to us. What about you? Have you had a time when you just sat and thought on God and then He talked to you?

Exercise

Let's follow David's example.

- ❏ Sit in a comfortable position.
- ❏ With a pencil and paper handy, sit and think about how God has forgiven you.
- ❏ What are you grateful for?
- ❏ As you think, begin to write your feelings down on paper.
- ❏ When you are finished writing, sit a while longer and begin to write any other thoughts that come to mind.
- ❏ Has God spoken back to you?
- ❏ Record your experience in your notebook.

Psalm 42 (A contemplation of the sons of Korah.)

Verses 1-4 (Longing for God.)

"As the deer pants for the water brooks, so pants my soul for You, O God. My soul thirsts for God, for the living God. When shall I come and appear before God? My tears have been my food day and night, while they continually say to me, 'Where is your God?' When I remember these things, I pour out my soul within me. For I used to go with the multitude; I went with them to the house of God, with the voice of joy and praise, with a multitude that kept a pilgrim feast."

Have you ever felt a longing for God, a time when you really wanted to be with Him? Let's follow the example of the sons of Korah for our next exercise.

Exercise

Make sure to have a pencil and paper handy.

- ❑ Get in a comfortable position.
- ❑ Think on how much you love God, how much you long to be with Him.
- ❑ Begin to write your feelings on paper.
- ❑ When you are finished, record your experience in your notebook.

Psalm 73 (A Psalm of Asaph)

Verses 1-3 (Transparent with God)

"Truly God is good to Israel, to such as are pure in heart. But as for me, my feet had almost stumbled; my steps had nearly slipped. For I was envious of the boastful, when I saw the prosperity of the wicked."

Verses 13-17 (His transparency continues.)

"Surely I have cleansed my heart in vain, and washed my hands in innocence. For all day long I have been plagued, and chastened every morning. If I had said, 'I will speak thus,' behold, I would have been untrue to the generation of Your

children. When I thought how to understand this, it was too painful for me—Until I went into the sanctuary of God; then I understood their end."

Do you have a hard time being transparent with God? Are you hiding something you are angry about, something you think isn't fair? Let's make this the subject of our next exercise.

Exercise: (Have a pencil and paper handy.)

- ❏ Sit in a comfortable position.
- ❏ Think about something you have felt unable or unwilling to talk to God about.
- ❏ Begin to write your feelings down.
- ❏ Can you share them with God now?
- ❏ Write your experience in your notebook.

Psalm 89 (A contemplation of Ethan the Ezraphite.)

Verses 1-2 (Praise for God)

I will sing of the mercies of the Lord forever; with my mouth I will make known Your faithfulness to all generations. For I have said, 'Mercy shall be built up forever; Your faithfulness You shall establish in the very heavens'."

Notice how he believes God and loves Him for his faithfulness. How has God shown Himself faithful in your life? Let's make this the subject of our next exercise.

Exercise

Make sure to have a pencil and paper handy.

- ❏ Get in a comfortable position.
- ❏ Sit and think on how God has shown Himself faithful to you.
- ❏ Begin to write out your thoughts on His faithfulness.
- ❏ After you are done writing, sit for a moment.
- ❏ Begin to write any thoughts that come to mind.
- ❏ Record your experience in your notebook.

Psalm 90 (Prayer of Moses.)

Verses 1-2 (Telling God who He is)

"Lord, you have been our dwelling place in all generations. Before the mountains were brought forth, or ever You had formed the earth and the world, even from everlasting to everlasting, You are God."

Who is God to you? Who has He shown Himself to be in your life? We will make that the subject of our next exercise.

Exercise

Be sure to have a pencil and paper handy.

- ❑ Get in a comfortable position.
- ❑ Think about God and who He is.
- ❑ Think about who He has been to you personally.
- ❑ After you have thought about it for a while, begin to write your thoughts down.
- ❑ When you are finished, sit quietly for a moment.
- ❑ Write down what is going on in your mind.
- ❑ Record your experience in your notebook.

My Favorite Mystic of Old

The writings of Madame Guyon have been very influential in my life. She lived from 1648-1717 and was branded a heretic in 1688 for teaching her methods of prayer. Her critics today say that she taught an experience of God rather than a biblical knowledge of God. But let's look at what she actually said. This portion is taken from her book, "Experiencing the Depths of Jesus Christ".

Page 117. "If a new convert were introduced to real prayer and to a true inward experience of Christ as soon as he became converted, you would see countless numbers of converts go on to become true disciples."

Page 118. "If you are in charge of new believers, lead them to a real inner knowledge of Jesus Christ."

Page 119. "You who are in authority over young believers must yourself one day give an account to God for those who have been entrusted to you by the Lord. You will have to give an account for not having discovered for yourself this hidden treasure—this inner relationship to Christ—and you will also be held accountable for not having given that treasure to those in your charge."

Page 119 "Nor will you, in that day be able to excuse yourself by saying that this walk with the Lord was too dangerous or that simple, uneducated people are unable to understand spiritual things. The Scripture simply does not validate these conjectures."

Madame Guyon was not saying that we didn't need the Scriptures to know God. She was saying that in addition to that, we needed to know God, and to experience Him for ourselves, to know that He is alive within us. Scripture does bear this out. Luke 17:21 tells us that the kingdom of God is within us. John 14:23 (NKJV) says in part, "We will come and make Our home with him". John 15:4 (NKJV) says "Abide in Me, and I in you. As the branch cannot bear fruit of itself, unless it abides in the vine, neither can you, unless you abide in Me."

Madame Guyon taught two ways of meeting with God through the Scriptures. Both are also found in, "Experiencing the Depths of Jesus Christ".

1. Praying the Scriptures—involves both reading and prayer.

Page 7.

"Turn to the Scripture; choose some passage that is simple and fairly practical. Next, come to the Lord. Come quietly and humbly. There, before Him, read a small portion of the passage of Scripture you have opened to.

Be careful as you read. Take in fully, gently and carefully what you are reading. Taste it and digest it as you read."

Page 8.

"You may then want to take that portion of Scripture that has touched you and turn it into prayer."

"After you have sensed something of the passage and after you know that the essence of that portion has been extracted and all the deeper sense of it is gone, then, very slowly, gently, and in a calm manner begin to read the next portion of the passage. You will be surprised to find that when your time with the Lord has ended, you will have read very little, probably no more than half a page."

Her critics also say she looked for God within herself, rather than without. That is a half-truth, as you can see from her writings. Madame used Scripture to meet with God, spirit to Spirit.

2.   Beholding the Lord

Page 9.

"In 'beholding the Lord,' you come to the Lord in a totally different way. Perhaps at this point I need to share with you the greatest difficulty you will have in waiting upon the Lord. It has to do with your mind. The mind has a very strong tendency to stray away from the Lord."

*"Therefore, as you come before your Lord to sit in His presence, beholding Him, make use of the Scripture to **quiet your mind**. The way to do it is really quite simple. First, read a passage of Scripture. Once you sense the Lord's presence, the content of what you have read is no longer important."*

Page 10.

"The Scripture has served its purpose; it has quieted your mind; it has brought you to Him. You begin by setting aside a time to be with the Lord. When you do come to Him, come quietly. Turn your heart to the presence of God. How is this done? This too is quite simple. You turn to Him by faith. By faith you believe you have come into the presence of God."

"Next, while you are before the Lord, begin to read some portion of Scripture."

"As you read, pause."

"The pause should be quite gentle. You have pause so that you may set your mind on the Spirit. You have set your mind inwardly on Christ."

And so, Madame Guyon tells how to behold the Lord in our spirit. What do Scriptures say about this? Romans 7:22 says, "For I delight in the law of God according to the inward man." Psalm 4:4 says to meditate within your heart on your bed, and be still. There are many other Scriptures on this in the ones I gave you for meditation. If you're not convinced, use a concordance to look other Scriptures up. Using Scripture to meet with God is scriptural.

The Catholic Encyclopedia calls this type of prayer the "Prayer of Quiet." In this type of prayer, it says that the soul experiences an extraordinary peace and rest, accompanied by delight or pleasure in contemplating God as present. In the prayer, God gives to the soul an intellectual knowledge of His presence, and makes it feel that it is really in communication with Him, although He does this in a somewhat obscure manner. It goes on to say that at first the prayer of quiet is given from time to time, and merely for a few minutes. It takes place when the soul has already arrived at the prayer of recollection and silence, or what some authors call the prayer of simplicity. A time often comes when the prayer of quiet is not only very frequent, but habitual. In this case it occurs not only at the time set for prayer, but every time that the thought of God presents itself. Even then it is subject to interruptions and alterations of intensity, sometimes strong, sometimes weak. The encyclopedia also says the spiritual fruits are an interior peace which remains after the time of prayer, profound humility, aptitude and a disposition for spiritual duties, a heavenly light in the intellect, and stability of the will in goodness. [The Catholic Encyclopedia, Volume XII Online Edition]

Exercises

Follow Madame Guyon's advice. First use the "Praying the Scriptures" example for meeting with God through the Scriptures. Then use the "Beholding the Lord" example for the second one. Record your experiences in your notebook.

"The Way of a Pilgrim" and "The Pilgrim Continues His Way" translated by Olga Savin

The breathing prayer is the same as what some call the Jesus Prayer. This was an early attempt to fulfill the Scripture of being able to pray without ceasing. In "The Way of the Pilgrim", it gives us a look at how this prayer began and spread. It is an attempt to continually keep Jesus on your mind,

His word in your mouth and in your spirit, first, last and always. People continue to practice this type of prayer today. Many call it meditative prayer or contemplative prayer.

How Best To Say The Jesus Prayer

"You know that our breathing is the inhaling and exhaling of air. The organ that serves for this is the lungs that lie round the heart, so that the air passing through them thereby envelops the heart. Thus, breathing is a natural way to the heart. And so, having collected your mind within you, lead it into the channel of breathing through which air reaches the heart and, together with this inhaled air, force your mind to descend into the heart and to remain there. Accustom it not to come out of the heart too soon, for at first it feels very lonely in that inner seclusion and imprisonment. But when it gets accustomed to it, it begins on the contrary to dislike its aimless circling outside, for it is no longer unpleasant and wearisome for it to be within. Just as a man who has been away from home when he returns is beside himself with joy at seeing again his children and wife, embraces them and cannot talk to them enough, so the mind, when it unites with the heart, is filled with unspeakable joy and delight. Then a man sees that the Kingdom of Heaven is truly within us; and seeing it now in himself, he strives with pure prayer to keep it and strengthen it there."

"When you thus enter into the place of the heart, as I have shown you, give thanks to God and, praising his mercy, keep always to do this doing, and it will teach you things that in no other way you will ever learn. Moreover you should know that when your mind becomes firmly established in the heart, it must remain there silent and idle, but it should constantly repeat the Jesus prayer: 'Lord Jesus Christ, Son of God have mercy upon me!' and never cease. For this practice, keeping the mind from dreams, renders it elusive and impenetrable to enemy suggestions and every day leads it more and more to love and longing for God." Nicephorus the Solitary. The next chapter will deal with a practical method of developing your relationship with God.

SECTION FOUR

*30 Days To Developing
Your Awareness*

CHAPTER ELEVEN

AWARENESS DEVELOPMENT EXERCISES

DAY ONE

Being Present To The Moment

- ❏ Take a deep breath and let it out slowly. Now notice,
- ❏ What do you hear?
- ❏ What do you smell?
- ❏ What do you see?
- ❏ What do you feel?
- ❏ What do you taste?
- ❏ What is going through your mind?

Now

- ❏ Listen, what do you hear? How do you hear it?
- ❏ Take a deep breath. What do you smell? How do you smell it?
- ❏ Look around you. What do you see? How do you see it?
- ❏ What do you feel? How do you feel it?
- ❏ What do you taste? How do you taste it?
- ❏ What is going through your mind?
- ❏ Record your answers in your notebook.

DAY TWO

Present To the Moment 2

- ❏ Take a deep breath and let it out slowly.
- ❏ Take a moment to notice everything you are thinking, hearing, and sensing.
- ❏ Now ask God a specific question, for instance, "How can I show you how much I love You?". After you ask the question, begin recording what comes to your mind.
- ❏ Record your experience in your notebook.

DAY THREE

- ❏ Take a deep breath and let it out slowly.
- ❏ Take a moment to notice what you are feeling, thinking and hearing.
- ❏ Ask God to speak to you through the Scriptures.
- ❏ Read a passage of Scripture until the Holy Spirit draws you to a particular verse, phrase or word.
- ❏ Write out what you feel God is saying to you through it.
- ❏ Record your experience in your notebook.

DAY FOUR

- ❏ Take a deep breath and let it out slowly.
- ❏ Notice what you smell.
- ❏ Notice what you hear.
- ❏ Notice what you are thinking.
- ❏ Notice what emotions you're feeling and what memories the emotions bring.
- ❏ Record your experience in your notebook.

DAY FIVE

Throughout the day take a few minutes to allow your spirit to sense any information you need to know from the Holy Spirit, without asking any specific questions. Simply wait to see if there is anything in your spirit to give you the information you need for the day. Record your experience in your notebook.

DAY SIX

- ☐ Take a deep breath and let it out slowly.
- ☐ Notice what you are seeing, hearing, and sensing at this moment.
- ☐ After reading this, look up and take the first thing your eyes settle on and describe it in detail.
- ☐ Now, ask God to speak to you through what you see.
- ☐ What do you sense? What feelings, images or story do you get?
- ☐ Record your impressions in your notebook.

DAY SEVEN

- ☐ Take a deep breath and let it out slowly.
- ☐ Notice everything you are seeing, sensing, hearing, and what is going through your mind.
- ☐ After a moment allow yourself to stop when a memory comes to mind.
- ☐ Write down the memory.
- ☐ Do this for three or four memories.
- ☐ Is there a common thread to the memories?
- ☐ What do these memories say to you?
- ☐ Record your impressions in your notebook.

WEEKLY SPIRITUAL EXERCISE
PUTTING IT ALL TOGETHER

1. Look at all your notes from the exercises you did this week.
2. What do your answers have in common?

   ❏ What overall themes emerge? Don't look simply for the obvious. Some can be quite inconspicuous. _____ _____ _____

   ❏ If they don't seem to go together, does this bring out things that concern you or things that you have wanted answers to? _____ _____

   ❏ In what ways are they similar? _____ _____ _____

3. What do they tell you about what God is saying to you? What areas of your life is He speaking to? _____ _____ _____

4. Did this answer any questions you've had on your mind? _____ _____ _____

5. Did this bring up any new questions you'd like answers to? _____ _____ _____ _____ _____

TESTING WHAT YOU'RE GETTING

(Images, Thoughts, Impressions)

When asking God for His leading, these are areas we need to be especially cautious. Check to see if the word or guidance you receive is any of the following:

- ❑ Something you intensely desire.
- ❑ Something you really don't want to happen.
- ❑ Anything that is a substitute for an intimate relationship with God.
- ❑ Something that lifts up you, not God.

Adapted from "How To Hear God's Voice" by Mark and Patti Virkler
Available at www.cwgministries.org
(used with permission)

Find Its Origin, Test Its Content & Check Its Fruit 1 John 4:1,5;
Matthew 7:16

SELF	GOD	ANOTHER SPIRIT
Comes from the mind/a progressive building of ideas. My wants, desires, & thoughts.	Pictures and thoughts come from the inner—most being. Sensed in spirit, then formed.	Comes from the mind. A picture or thought.
May be good or bad. Consideration of things I have learned. May or may not want to test it.	Instructive, uplifting, comforting & peaceful, Not afraid of testing.	Negative, destructive, pushy, fearful, anxious, unsettled, exhaustion, condemnation. Afraid of being tested.
Results vary.	Quickens faith, peace, good fruit, knowledge, enlightenment, strength & humility.	Fear, compulsion, bondage, anxiety, confusion, inflated ego.

DAY EIGHT

- ❑ Take a deep breath and let it out slowly.
- ❑ What are your five physical senses perceiving right now?
- ❑ What is your overall mood?
- ❑ How does your body feel?
- ❑ Is there a prominent emotion you are feeling?
- ❑ What is going through your mind?
- ❑ Be still for a moment.
- ❑ Ask God if there is anything He'd like to say to you.
- ❑ Record your results in your notebook.

DAY NINE

- ❑ Make it a habit to note everything you are thinking about throughout the day.
- ❑ Notice the things you've been thinking about continually in the last few hours, days, and months.
- ❑ Do you see a pattern?
- ❑ Your spirit is always giving you information to help you.
- ❑ What questions are you asking? What questions should you be asking?
- ❑ Record your answers in your notebook.

DAY TEN

- ❑ Take a deep breath and let it out slowly.
- ❑ When you look up from reading this, answer the following:
- ❑ What is the first thing you see? Describe it in detail.
- ❑ How would you like to change it?
- ❑ Where would it look best?
- ❑ What would you like to do with it?
- ❑ Why do you think you noticed this item?
- ❑ Record your answers in your notebook.

DAY ELEVEN

- ❑ Throughout the day take a few moments to become consciously aware of everything you notice.

❑ Out loud, report everything you observe continuously without interruption. This will give you practice for when giving a prophetic word to others.
❑ Record your experience in your notebook.

DAY TWELVE

❑ Take a deep breath and let it out slowly.
❑ Take a moment to notice what you're thinking, sensing, and hearing.

Throughout the day anytime you make contact with another person, notice the first few perceptions you have about this person. Record your experience in your notebook.

DAY THIRTEEN

❑ Take a deep breath and let it out slowly.
❑ Take a moment to notice what you're thinking, sensing, and hearing.

Throughout the day anytime you make contact with another person take a moment and perceive what they need at the moment. Ask God if there is anything He would like you to pray for them. Record your experience in your notebook.

DAY FOURTEEN

❑ Take a deep breath and let it out slowly.
❑ Take a moment to notice what you're thinking, sensing, and hearing.
❑ Focus on a specific question you'd like the Holy Spirit to answer for you.
❑ Notice the first impressions you receive.
❑ Interpret your impressions in light of your question.
❑ Verify your conclusions.
❑ Record your impressions in your notebook.

WEEKLY SPIRITUAL EXERCISE
PUTTING IT ALL TOGETHER

1. Look at all your notes from the exercises you did this week.
2. What do your answers have in common?

   ❑ What overall themes emerge? Don't look simply for the obvious. Some can be quite inconspicuous. _____
   _____
   _____

   ❑ If they don't seem to go together, does this bring out things that concern you or things that you have wanted answers to?
   _____
   _____

   ❑ In what ways are they similar? _____
   _____
   _____

3. What do they tell you about what God is saying to you? What areas of your life is He speaking to? _____
   _____
   _____

4. Did this answer any questions you've had on your mind?
   _____
   _____
   _____

5. Did this bring up any new questions you'd like answers to?
   _____
   _____
   _____
   _____
   _____

TESTING WHAT YOU'RE GETTING

(Images, Thoughts, Impressions)

When asking God for His leading, these are areas we need to be especially cautious. Check to see if the word or guidance you receive is any of the following:

- ❑ Something you intensely desire.
- ❑ Something you really don't want to happen.
- ❑ Anything that is a substitute for an intimate relationship with God.
- ❑ Something that lifts up you, not God.

Adapted from "How To Hear God's Voice" by Mark & Patti Virkler
Available at www.cwgministries.org
(used with permission)

Find Its Origin, Test Its Content & Check Its Fruit 1 John 4:1,5;
Matthew 7:16

SELF	GOD	ANOTHER SPIRIT
Comes from the mind/a progressive building of ideas. My wants, desires, & thoughts.	Pictures and thoughts come from the inner—most being. Sensed in spirit, then formed.	Comes from the mind. A picture or thought.
May be good or bad. Consideration of things I have learned. May or may not want to test it.	Instructive, uplifting, comforting & peaceful, Not afraid of testing.	Negative, destructive, pushy, fearful, anxious, unsettled, exhaustion, condemnation. Afraid of being tested.
Results vary.	Quickens faith, peace, good fruit, knowledge, enlightenment, strength & humility.	Fear, compulsion, bondage, anxiety, confusion, inflated ego.

DAY FIFTEEN

- ❑ Take a deep breath and let it out slowly.
- ❑ Notice what you are seeing, hearing, and sensing right now.
- ❑ Ask God to speak to you through the Scriptures. Read a passage of Scripture until you are drawn by the Holy Spirit to a particular verse, phrase, or word. Write down the Scripture. Write out what God is saying to you through it.
- ❑ Record it all in your notebook.

DAY SIXTEEN

- ❑ Take a deep breath and let it out slowly.
- ❑ Take a moment to notice what you are seeing, sensing, and hearing.
- ❑ Get still before the Lord.
- ❑ Don't ask anything, just sit in His presence.
- ❑ Stay that way for a while.
- ❑ Tell Him how much you love Him.
- ❑ When you are finished, record your experience in your notebook.

DAY SEVENTEEN

- ❑ Take a deep breath and let it out slowly.
- ❑ Take a moment to notice what you're seeing, hearing, and sensing.
- ❑ Ask the Holy Spirit a question.
- ❑ With a tape recorder going, report out loud everything you are sensing, hearing, and thinking.
- ❑ Report everything, do not edit or hold back anything.
- ❑ Record it in your notebook.
- ❑ As you look at it, what did the Holy Spirit say in response to your question?
- ❑ Record it in your notebook.

DAY EIGHTEEN

- ❑ Take a deep breath and let it out slowly.
- ❑ Pay attention to what you are hearing, sensing, tasting, seeing, and thinking.

❑ When you are finished, ask God if there is anything He would like to say to you.

❑ Start recording everything that comes to your mind.

❑ Record your experience in your notebook.

DAY NINETEEN

❑ Take a deep breath and let it out slowly.

❑ Now notice and speak out loud:
What do you see?
What do you hear?
What do you feel?
What do you taste?
What do you smell?

❑ Record your answers in your notebook.

DAY TWENTY

❑ Take a deep breath and let it out slowly.

❑ Notice what you are thinking, sensing, seeing, and hearing.

❑ Read a passage of Scripture until God stops you.

❑ Meditate on that portion of Scripture.

❑ Record what God is showing to you.

DAY TWENTY-ONE

❑ Take a deep breath and let it out slowly.

❑ Notice what you are thinking, sensing, seeing, and hearing.

❑ Choose a close friend to pray for.

❑ Ask God to give you something that will uplift them.

❑ Read a portion of Scripture until God stops you.

❑ Record it in your notebook.

❑ Ask God how He wants you to share the uplifting message with them that was given, (written or verbal).

❑ Record your experience in your notebook and follow His direction.

WEEKLY SPIRITUAL EXERCISE
PUTTING IT ALL TOGETHER

1. Look at all your notes from the exercises you did this week.
2. What do your answers have in common?

   ❑ What overall themes emerge? Don't look simply for the obvious. Some can be quite inconspicuous. _____

   _____

   _____

   ❑ If they don't seem to go together, does this bring out things that concern you or things that you have wanted answers to?

   _____

   _____

   ❑ In what ways are they similar? _____

   _____

   _____

3. What do they tell you about what God is saying to you? What areas of your life is He speaking to? _____

   _____

   _____

4. Did this answer any questions you've had on your mind?

   _____

   _____

   _____

5. Did this bring up any new questions you'd like answers to?

   _____

   _____

   _____

   _____

TESTING WHAT YOU'RE GETTING

(Images, Thoughts, Impressions)

When asking God for His leading, these are areas we need to be especially cautious. Check to see if the word or guidance you receive is any of the following:

☐ Something you intensely desire.
☐ Something you really don't want to happen.
☐ Anything that is a substitute for an intimate relationship with God.
☐ Something that lifts up you, not God.

Adapted from "How To Hear God's Voice" by Mark & Patti Virkler
Available at www.cwgministries.org
(used with permission)

Find Its Origin, Test Its Content & Check Its Fruit 1 John 4:1,5;
Matthew 7:16

SELF	GOD	ANOTHER SPIRIT
Comes from the mind/a progressive building of ideas. My wants, desires, & thoughts.	Pictures and thoughts come from the inner—most being. Sensed in spirit, then formed.	Comes from the mind. A picture or thought.
May be good or bad. Consideration of things I have learned. May or may not want to test it.	Instructive, uplifting, comforting & peaceful, Not afraid of testing.	Negative, destructive, pushy, fearful, anxious, unsettled, exhaustion, condemnation. Afraid of being tested.
Results vary.	Quickens faith, peace, good fruit, knowledge, enlightenment, strength & humility.	Fear, compulsion, bondage, anxiety, confusion, inflated ego.

DAY TWENTY-TWO

- ❏ Take a deep breath and exhale slowly.
- ❏ Take a few minutes to notice what you are seeing, hearing, sensing, and what is going through your mind.
- ❏ Ask God to show you a Scripture He wants to make real to you.
- ❏ Meditate on it.
- ❏ Record your insights and reactions in your notebook.

DAY TWENTY-THREE

- ❏ Take a deep breath and let it out slowly.
- ❏ Take a few minutes to notice what you're seeing, hearing, sensing, and what is going through your mind.
- ❏ Slowly read a passage of Scripture, looking for a word or phrase that draws your attention.
- ❏ When you find it, close your eyes and repeat it silently.
- ❏ As you do, what comes to mind? (Memories, words, feelings or even smells that are associated with the word or the phrase you're drawn to.)
- ❏ Record your response in your notebook.

DAY TWENTY-FOUR

- ❏ Take a deep breath and exhale slowly.
- ❏ Notice what you are sensing, seeing, hearing, and smelling.
- ❏ Notice what is going through your mind.
- ❏ Begin to read 1 John 1. Read the passage slowly.
- ❏ What word, phrase, or passage of Scripture captures your attention?
- ❏ Record your thoughts in your notebook.
- ❏ Now upon reflection, why do you think it's important?
- ❏ What is the Holy Spirit saying to you?
- ❏ Record your answers in your notebook.

DAY TWENTY-FIVE

- ❏ Take a deep breath and exhale slowly.
- ❏ Notice what is going through your mind, what you're seeing, what you're sensing, and what you're hearing.

- ❏ Take some time to think about why you love God.
- ❏ Express your love to Him.
- ❏ What is His response to you?
- ❏ Record your experience in your notebook.

DAY TWENTY-SIX

- ❏ Take a deep breath and exhale slowly.
- ❏ Take a moment to notice what's going through your mind, what you're seeing, feeling, sensing, and hearing.
- ❏ Describe the outfit you are wearing in detail.
- ❏ Allow God to speak to you through it.
- ❏ Record your impressions in your notebook.

DAY TWENTY-SEVEN

- ❏ Take a deep breath and exhale slowly.
- ❏ Take a moment to notice what you are seeing, hearing, and sensing.
- ❏ Ask God if there is anything He would like to say to you.
- ❏ Speak out whatever comes to your mind.
- ❏ Record your experience in your notebook.

DAY TWENTY-EIGHT

- ❏ Take a deep breath and let it out slowly.
- ❏ Take a moment to notice what you're seeing, hearing, and sensing.
- ❏ Ask the Holy Spirit to help you be present to the moment with others.
- ❏ Now call or meet with someone.
- ❏ Ask them a question and listen to their answers.
- ❏ If you find yourself not paying attention, bring your attention back to them.
- ❏ Continually in your spirit, be open to whatever God may want to say.
- ❏ Record your experiences in your notebook.

WEEKLY SPIRITUAL EXERCISE
PUTTING IT ALL TOGETHER

1. Look at all your notes from the exercises you did this week.
2. What do your answers have in common?

   ❑ What overall themes emerge? Don't look simply for the obvious. Some
   can be quite inconspicuous. _____
   _____
   _____

   ❑ If they don't seem to go together, does this bring out things that
   concern you or things that you have wanted answers to?
   _____
   _____

   ❑ In what ways are they similar? _____
   _____
   _____

3. What do they tell you about what God is saying to you? What areas of
   your life is He speaking to? _____
   _____
   _____

4. Did this answer any questions you've had on your mind?
   _____
   _____
   _____

5. Did this bring up any new questions you'd like answers to?
   _____
   _____
   _____
   _____

TESTING WHAT YOU'RE GETTING

(Images, Thoughts, Impressions)

When asking God for His leading, these are areas we need to be especially cautious. Check to see if the word or guidance you receive is any of the following:

- ☐ Something you intensely desire.
- ☐ Something you really don't want to happen.
- ☐ Anything that is a substitute for an intimate relationship with God.
- ☐ Something that lifts up you, not God.

Adapted from "How To Hear God's Voice" by Mark & Patti Virkler
Available at www.cwgministries.org
(used with permission)

Find Its Origin, Test Its Content & Check Its Fruit 1 John 4:1,5; Matthew 7:16

SELF	GOD	ANOTHER SPIRIT
Comes from the mind/a progressive building of ideas. My wants, desires, & thoughts.	Pictures and thoughts come from the inner—most being. Sensed in spirit, then formed.	Comes from the mind. A picture or thought.
May be good or bad. Consideration of things I have learned. May or may not want to test it.	Instructive, uplifting, comforting & peaceful, Not afraid of testing.	Negative, destructive, pushy, fearful, anxious, unsettled, exhaustion, condemnation. Afraid of being tested.
Results vary.	Quickens faith, peace, good fruit, knowledge, enlightenment, strength & humility.	Fear, compulsion, bondage, anxiety, confusion, inflated ego.

DAY TWENTY-NINE

- ❑ Take a deep breath and exhale slowly.
- ❑ Notice what you are seeing, hearing, sensing, and what is going through your mind.
- ❑ Meditate on this:

1 John 2:20 (NKJV)
"But you have an anointing from the Holy One and you know all things."

- ❑ Say, "I have an anointing from the Holy One and I know all things".
- ❑ Ask God to show you how real this is.
- ❑ Ask Him for His knowledge and wisdom.
- ❑ Record your impressions in your notebook.

DAY THIRTY

- ❑ Take a deep breath and exhale slowly.
- ❑ Notice what you're thinking, hearing, seeing, and sensing.
- ❑ Read 1 John 2:20 again today.
- ❑ Reflect on this verse, allowing it to illuminate your intimate relationship with the Holy Spirit and the anointing He has given you.
- ❑ As you do, what do you see?
- ❑ What do you hear?
- ❑ What do you feel?
- ❑ What is going through your mind?
- ❑ Record your experience in your notebook.

WEEKLY SPIRITUAL EXERCISE
PUTTING IT ALL TOGETHER

1. Look at all your notes from the exercises you did this week.
2. What do your answers have in common?

   ❑ What overall themes emerge? Don't look simply for the obvious. Some can be quite inconspicuous. _____

   _____

   _____

   ❑ If they don't seem to go together, does this bring out things that concern you or things that you have wanted answers to?

   _____

   _____

   ❑ In what ways are they similar? _____

   _____

   _____

3. What do they tell you about what God is saying to you? What areas of your life is He speaking to? _____

   _____

   _____

4. Did this answer any questions you've had on your mind?

   _____

   _____

   _____

5. Did this bring up any new questions you'd like answers to?

   _____

   _____

   _____

   _____

   _____

TESTING WHAT YOU'RE GETTING

(Images, Thoughts, Impressions)

When asking God for His leading, these are areas we need to be especially cautious. Check to see if the word or guidance you receive is any of the following:

- ❑ Something you intensely desire.
- ❑ Something you really don't want to happen.
- ❑ Anything that is a substitute for an intimate relationship with God.
- ❑ Something that lifts up you, not God.

Adapted from "How To Hear God's Voice" by Mark & Patti Virkler
Available at www.cwgministries.org
(used with permission)

Find Its Origin, Test Its Content & Check Its Fruit 1 John 4:1,5; Matthew 7:16

SELF	GOD	ANOTHER SPIRIT
Comes from the mind/a progressive building of ideas. My wants, desires, & thoughts.	Pictures and thoughts come from the inner— most being. Sensed in spirit, then formed.	Comes from the mind. A picture or thought.
May be good or bad. Consideration of things I have learned. May or may not want to test it.	Instructive, uplifting, comforting & peaceful, Not afraid of testing.	Negative, destructive, pushy, fearful, anxious, unsettled, exhaustion, condemnation. Afraid of being tested.
Results vary.	Quickens faith, peace, good fruit, knowledge, enlightenment, strength & humility.	Fear, compulsion, bondage, anxiety, confusion, inflated ego.

CHAPTER TWELVE

QUICK EXERCISES FOR

AWARENESS DEVELOPMENT

❑ After you read this, close your eyes and take a deep breath through your nose and let it out through you mouth. What is going through your mind?

❑ Take a deep breath and let it out slowly through your mouth. Right now, what do you feel inside?

❑ Relax your shoulders and neck. Take a deep breath and let it out slowly through your mouth. What do you smell? What do you see? What do you hear?

❑ How do you know Jesus loves you? Describe the first thing that comes to your mind.

❑ Take a deep breath and allow yourself to relax. Notice what you smell. Notice what you hear. Notice what you are thinking.

❑ Allow yourself to notice what emotion you're feeling in this moment. Does it make you think of a certain memory?

❑ Take a deep breath and exhale slowly. Allow your spirit to sense any information you need to know right now. Simply wait and see if there is anything that comes to your mind. What is it?

❑ After you read this, allow yourself to notice what you are remembering. What is the memory or feeling you are having? Now continue to the next feeling or memory. What is it?

❑ Take a few seconds to notice how your body feels. Describe it. What kind of mood are you in? Describe it. What thoughts or memories are going on in your mind?

❑ What have you been thinking about a lot in the last few hours? What questions are you asking?

❑ Out loud say everything that comes to your attention, be it sounds, smells, feelings or thoughts.

SECTION FIVE

Practicing The Prophetic

CHAPTER THIRTEEN

PRACTICING GIVING A PROPHETIC WORD

DAY ONE

Please get out paper and a pen or pencil, as well as three envelopes. Now spend a few minutes relaxing your body. Take a deep breath and exhale slowly through your mouth.

- ❑ Ask God to show you three people He would like you to pray for.
- ❑ Write down the names of the three people He shows you on separate sheets of paper.
- ❑ Fold up the paper so you cannot see the names.
- ❑ Place each one into its own envelope.
- ❑ Mix the envelopes up.
- ❑ Number the envelopes.
- ❑ Choose an envelope and take a sheet of paper and write the number of that envelope on top of the sheet of paper.
- ❑ Now relax again, and without opening the envelope begin praying for the person. When you are finished, write on the paper what you prayed over the person.
- ❑ Write out anything you saw when you were praying, anything you sensed, and anything you may have heard. Place the papers and envelopes in your notebook.

DAY TWO

- ❑ Choose a different envelope and take a sheet of paper and write the number of that envelope on top of the sheet of paper.
- ❑ Now relax, take a deep breath, and exhale slowly.
- ❑ Begin praying for the person without opening the envelope. When you are finished praying, write on the paper what you prayed over the person.
- ❑ Write out anything you saw when you were praying, anything you sensed, and anything you may have heard. Place the paper in your notebook.

DAY THREE

- ❑ Choose the last envelope not prayed over and take a sheet of paper and write the number of that envelope on top of the sheet of paper.
- ❑ Now relax, take a deep breath, and exhale slowly.
- ❑ Begin praying for the person without opening the envelope. When you are finished praying, write on the paper what you prayed over the person.
- ❑ Write out anything you saw when you were praying, anything you sensed, and anything you may have heard. Place the paper in your notebook.

DAY FOUR

- ❑ Choose an envelope and again on a sheet of paper, write the number of the envelope.
- ❑ Now relax, take a deep breath, and exhale slowly.
- ❑ Begin praying for the person without opening the envelope. When you are finished praying, write on the paper what you prayed over the person.
- ❑ Write out anything you saw when you were praying, anything you sensed, and anything you may have heard. Place the paper in your notebook.

DAY FIVE

- ❑ Choose an envelope and again on a sheet of paper, write the number of the envelope.
- ❑ Now relax, take a deep breath, and exhale slowly.

❑ Begin praying for the person without opening the envelope. When you are finished praying, write on the paper what you prayed over the person.

❑ Write out anything you saw when you were praying, anything you sensed, and anything you may have heard. Place the paper in your notebook.

DAY SIX

❑ Choose the last envelope and again, on a sheet of paper write the number of the envelope.

❑ Now relax, take a deep breath, and exhale slowly.

❑ Begin praying for the person without opening the envelope. When you are finished praying, write on the paper what you prayed over the person.

❑ Write out anything you saw when you were praying, anything you sensed, and anything you may have heard. Place the paper in your notebook.

DAY SEVEN

❑ Take out three sheets of paper. On the top of each write a corresponding envelope number.

❑ Choose an envelope.

❑ Relax. Take a deep breath and exhale slowly.

❑ Ask the Holy Spirit what He would like to say to this person.

❑ Begin writing. If you're not getting anything, begin to write everything you are thinking, sensing, and hearing.

❑ If you feel you aren't thinking, sensing, or hearing anything of value, go ahead and pretend you are making something up. Say, "I know I'm not sensing anything, but if I were, it would be . . ." This is practice, after all.

❑ Do the same for the other two envelopes.

❑ Use the following sheets to check what you've done.

❑ When you're finished, based on your results, you can decide whether to share with the individuals or not.

WEEKLY SPIRITUAL EXERCISE
PUTTING IT ALL TOGETHER

1. Look at all your notes from the exercises you did this week.

    ❑ What overall themes emerge? Don't look simply for the obvious. Some
       can be quite inconspicuous. _____
       _____
       _____

    ❑ If they don't seem to go together, does this illuminate other things
       that may need prayer? _____
       _____
       _____

    ❑ In what ways are they similar? _____
       _____
       _____

2. What do they tell you about what God is saying? What areas of life is He
    speaking to? _____
    _____
    _____

3. How do you think you can best share this with the individual you've been
    praying for? _____
    _____
    _____
    _____

4. Do you plan to share this with them?
    _____
    _____
    _____
    _____

TESTING WHAT YOU'RE GETTING

(Images, Thoughts, Impressions)

When asking God for His leading, these are areas we need to be especially cautious. Check to see if the word or guidance you receive is any of the following:

- ☐ Something you intensely desire.
- ☐ Something you really don't want to happen.
- ☐ Anything that is a substitute for an intimate relationship with God.
- ☐ Something that lifts up you, not God.

Adapted from "How To Hear God's Voice" by Mark and Patty Virkler
Available at www.cwgministries.org
(used with permission)

Find Its Origin, Test Its Content & Check Its Fruit 1 John 4:1,5; Matthew 7:16

SELF	GOD	ANOTHER SPIRIT
Comes from the mind/a progressive building of ideas. My wants, desires, & thoughts.	Pictures and thoughts come from the inner—most being. Sensed in spirit, then formed.	Comes from the mind. A picture or thought.
May be good or bad. Consideration of things I have learned. May or may not want to test it.	Instructive, uplifting, comforting & peaceful, Not afraid of testing.	Negative, destructive, pushy, fearful, anxious, unsettled, exhaustion, condemnation. Afraid of being tested.
Results vary.	Quickens faith, peace, good fruit, knowledge, enlightenment, strength & humility.	Fear, compulsion, bondage, anxiety, confusion, inflated ego.

DAY EIGHT

Choose six names. Put them in envelopes the same way you did for last week. Mix them up and number them.

- ❑ Get out a sheet of paper, choose an envelope, and write the envelope's number on the paper.
- ❑ Get out your tape recorder and a blank tape.
- ❑ Relax. Take a deep breath and exhale slowly.
- ❑ Turn on the recorder and begin to prophesy over the person in the envelope. Speak out everything you are thinking, feeling, and seeing.
- ❑ Record in your notebook what is on the tape.

DAY NINE

- ❑ Get out a sheet of paper, choose an envelope, and write the envelope's number on the paper.
- ❑ Get out your tape recorder and a blank tape.
- ❑ Relax. Take a deep breath and exhale slowly.
- ❑ Turn on the recorder and begin to prophesy over the person in the envelope. Speak out everything you are thinking, feeling, and seeing.
- ❑ Record in your notebook what is on the tape.

DAY TEN

- ❑ Get out a sheet of paper, choose an envelope, and write the envelope's number on the paper.
- ❑ Get out your tape recorder and a blank tape.
- ❑ Relax. Take a deep breath and exhale slowly.
- ❑ Turn on the recorder and begin to prophesy over the person in the envelope. Speak out everything you are thinking, feeling, and seeing.
- ❑ Record in the notebook what is on the tape.

DAY ELEVEN

- ❑ Get out a sheet of paper, choose an envelope, and write the envelope's number on the paper.
- ❑ Get out your tape recorder and a blank tape.
- ❑ Relax. Take a deep breath and exhale slowly.

❑ Turn on the recorder and begin to prophesy over the person in the envelope. Speak out everything you are thinking, feeling, and seeing.

❑ Record in the notebook what is on the tape.

DAY TWELVE

❑ Get out a sheet of paper, choose an envelope, and write the envelope's number on the paper.

❑ Get out your tape recorder and a blank tape.

❑ Relax. Take a deep breath and exhale slowly.

❑ Turn on the recorder and begin to prophesy over the person in the envelope. Speak out everything you are thinking, feeling, and seeing.

❑ Record in the notebook what is on the tape.

DAY THIRTEEN

❑ Get out a sheet of paper, choose an envelope, and write the envelope's number on the paper.

❑ Get out your tape recorder and a blank tape.

❑ Relax. Take a deep breath and exhale slowly.

❑ Turn on the recorder and begin to prophesy over the person in the envelope. Speak out everything you are thinking, feeling, and seeing.

❑ Record in the notebook what is on the tape.

DAY FOURTEEN

❑ Today you will prophesy over each person's envelope. Prepare the sheets of paper.

❑ Get out your tape recorder and a blank tape for each envelope. Number the tapes to correspond to each envelope.

❑ Relax. Take a deep breath and exhale slowly.

❑ Turn on the recorder and begin to prophesy over the person in the first envelope. Speak out everything you are thinking, feeling, and seeing.

❑ Do this for each envelope.

❑ Record in the notebook what is recorded on the tape.

❑ Go over the sheets at the end of this chapter to put together and judge what you're getting.

WEEKLY SPIRITUAL EXERCISE
PUTTING IT ALL TOGETHER

1. Look at all your notes from the exercises you did this week.

    ❑ What overall themes emerge? Don't look simply for the obvious. Some can be quite inconspicuous. _____
    _____
    _____

    ❑ If they don't seem to go together, does this illuminate other things that may need prayer? _____
    _____
    _____

    ❑ In what ways are they similar? _____
    _____
    _____

2. What do they tell you about what God is saying? What areas of life is He speaking to? _____
    _____
    _____
    _____

3. How do you think you can best share this with the individual you've been praying for? _____
    _____
    _____
    _____
    _____

4. Do you plan to share this with them?
    _____
    _____
    _____
    _____

TESTING WHAT YOU'RE GETTING

(Images, Thoughts, Impressions)

When asking God for His leading, these are areas we need to be especially cautious. Check to see if the word or guidance you receive is any of the following:

- ❑ Something you intensely desire.
- ❑ Something you really don't want to happen.
- ❑ Anything that is a substitute for an intimate relationship with God.
- ❑ Something that lifts up you, not God.

Adapted from "How To Hear God's Voice" by Mark and Patty Virkler
Available at www.cwgministries.org
(used with permission)

Find Its Origin, Test Its Content & Check Its Fruit 1 John 4:1,5;
Matthew 7:16

SELF	GOD	ANOTHER SPIRIT
Comes from the mind/a progressive building of ideas. My wants, desires, & thoughts.	Pictures and thoughts come from the inner—most being. Sensed in spirit, then formed.	Comes from the mind. A picture or thought.
May be good or bad. Consideration of things I have learned. May or may not want to test it.	Instructive, uplifting, comforting & peaceful, Not afraid of testing.	Negative, destructive, pushy, fearful, anxious, unsettled, exhaustion, condemnation. Afraid of being tested.
Results vary.	Quickens faith, peace, good fruit, knowledge, enlightenment, strength & humility.	Fear, compulsion, bondage, anxiety, confusion, inflated ego.

DAY FIFTEEN

Get out a tape recorder and a blank tape.

- ❑ Ask the Holy Spirit a question you would like an answer to this week.
- ❑ Relax, take a deep breath and exhale slowly.
- ❑ Begin to speak out everything you are seeing and sensing, and what is going through your mind.
- ❑ Write your experience and what is on the tape in your notebook.

DAY SIXTEEN

- ❑ Watch a television program and ask God to speak to you through it.
- ❑ Record your impressions in your notebook.

DAY SEVENTEEN

- ❑ Listen to some music.
- ❑ Ask God to speak to you through it.
- ❑ Record your impressions in your notebook.

DAY EIGHTEEN

- ❑ Sit quietly for a moment.
- ❑ Reflect on the question you asked the Holy Spirit for this week. (Day fifteen).
- ❑ What thoughts are going through your mind?
- ❑ Record your impressions in your notebook.

DAY NINETEEN

- ❑ Relax, take a deep breath and exhale slowly.
- ❑ Imagine you are a part of your favorite Bible story. Who are you? What do you do? How does it make you feel?
- ❑ Describe your experience in your notebook.

DAY TWENTY

- ❑ Relax, take a deep breath and exhale slowly.
- ❑ Imagine you are in the crowd when Jesus is teaching. As you look at Him, what is He saying? How does it make you feel?
- ❑ Now, imagine that as He is talking, He is looking into your eyes. How does that affect you?
- ❑ Record your experience in your notebook.

DAY TWENTYONE

- ❑ Relax, take a deep breath and exhale slowly.
- ❑ Reflect once again on this week's question.
- ❑ What is going through your mind? What are you feeling? What are you hearing?
- ❑ Record your experience in your notebook.
- ❑ Now go over the sheets on the next two pages.

WEEKLY SPIRITUAL EXERCISE
PUTTING IT ALL TOGETHER

1. Look at all your notes from the exercises you did this week.

   ❑ What overall themes emerge? Don't look simply for the obvious. Some
   can be quite inconspicuous. _____
   _____
   _____

   ❑ If they don't seem to go together, does this illuminate other things
   that may need prayer? _____
   _____
   _____

   ❑ In what ways are they similar? _____
   _____
   _____

2. What do they tell you about what God is saying? What areas of life is He
   speaking to? _____
   _____
   _____
   _____

3. How do you think you can best share this with the individual you've been
   praying for? _____
   _____
   _____
   _____
   _____

4. Do you plan to share this with them?
   _____
   _____
   _____
   _____
   _____

TESTING WHAT YOU'RE GETTING

(Images, Thoughts, Impressions)

When asking God for His leading, these are areas we need to be especially cautious. Check to see if the word or guidance you receive is any of the following:

- ☐ Something you intensely desire.
- ☐ Something you really don't want to happen.
- ☐ Anything that is a substitute for an intimate relationship with God.
- ☐ Something that lifts up you, not God.

Adapted from "How To Hear God's Voice" by Mark and Patty Virkler
Available at www.cwgministries.org
(used with permission)

Find Its Origin, Test Its Content & Check Its Fruit 1 John 4:1,5;
Matthew 7:16

SELF	GOD	ANOTHER SPIRIT
Comes from the mind/a progressive building of ideas. My wants, desires, & thoughts.	Pictures and thoughts come from the inner— most being. Sensed in spirit, then formed.	Comes from the mind. A picture or thought.
May be good or bad. Consideration of things I have learned. May or may not want to test it.	Instructive, uplifting, comforting & peaceful, Not afraid of testing.	Negative, destructive, pushy, fearful, anxious, unsettled, exhaustion, condemnation. Afraid of being tested.
Results vary.	Quickens faith, peace, good fruit, knowledge, enlightenment, strength & humility.	Fear, compulsion, bondage, anxiety, confusion, inflated ego.

DAY TWENTY-TWO

Have three friends write out a question. It must be a simple and specific question. Have them seal the question in the envelope. Now mix the envelopes up. Number them. Tell your friends you'll get back with an answer in a week.

DAY TWENTY-THREE

- ❏ Get out a tape recorder and a blank tape.
- ❏ Relax, take a deep breath and exhale slowly.
- ❏ Choose one of the envelopes.
- ❏ Ask the Holy Spirit to give you the answer to the question.
- ❏ Begin to speak out everything you are seeing and sensing, and what is going through your mind.
- ❏ Write out what you received in your notebook.

DAY TWENTY-FOUR

- ❏ Get out a tape recorder and a blank tape.
- ❏ Relax, take a deep breath and exhale slowly.
- ❏ Choose one of the envelopes.
- ❏ Ask the Holy Spirit to give you the answer to the question.
- ❏ Begin to speak out everything you are seeing and sensing, and what is going through your mind.
- ❏ Write out what you received in your notebook.

DAY TWENTY-FIVE

- ❏ Get out a tape recorder and a blank tape.
- ❏ Relax, take a deep breath and exhale slowly.
- ❏ Choose one of the envelopes.
- ❏ Ask the Holy Spirit to give you the answer to the question.
- ❏ Begin to speak out everything you are seeing and sensing, and what is going through your mind.
- ❏ Write out what you received in your notebook.

DAY TWENTY-SIX

- ❏ Get out a tape recorder and a blank tape.

❑ Relax, take a deep breath and exhale slowly.
❑ Repeat the process with the same envelopes. Choose one of the envelopes.
❑ Ask the Holy Spirit to give you the answer to the question.
❑ Begin to speak out everything you are seeing and sensing, and what is going through your mind.
❑ Write out what you received in your notebook.

DAY TWENTY-SEVEN

❑ Get out a tape recorder and a blank tape.
❑ Relax, take a deep breath and exhale slowly.
❑ Choose one of the envelopes.
❑ Ask the Holy Spirit to give you the answer to the question.
❑ Begin to speak out everything you are seeing and sensing, and what is going through your mind.
❑ Write out what you received in your notebook.

DAY TWENTY-EIGHT

❑ Get out a tape recorder and a blank tape.
❑ Relax, take a deep breath and exhale slowly.
❑ Choose the last envelope.
❑ Ask the Holy Spirit to give you the answer to the question.
❑ Begin to speak out everything you are seeing and sensing, and what is going through you mind.
❑ Write out what you received in your notebook.

DAY TWENTY-NINE

Go over the sheets on the next two pages. Share the answers with your friends.

DAY THIRTY

Relax by just spending time with the Holy Spirit, reflecting on what you've learned. Continue to practice. Make up your own exercises. Enjoy God, and hearing His voice!

WEEKLY SPIRITUAL EXERCISE
PUTTING IT ALL TOGETHER

1. Look at all your notes from the exercises you did this week.

    ❑ What overall themes emerge? Don't look simply for the obvious. Some can be quite inconspicuous. _____
    _____
    _____

    ❑ If they don't seem to go together, does this illuminate other things that may need prayer? _____
    _____
    _____

    ❑ In what ways are they similar? _____
    _____
    _____

2. What do they tell you about what God is saying? What areas of life is He speaking to? _____
    _____
    _____
    _____

3. How do you think you can best share this with the individual you've been praying for? _____
    _____
    _____
    _____
    _____

4. Do you plan to share this with them?
    _____
    _____
    _____
    _____
    _____

TESTING WHAT YOU'RE GETTING

(Images, Thoughts, Impressions)

When asking God for His leading, these are areas we need to be especially cautious. Check to see if the word or guidance you receive is any of the following:

- ❏ Something you intensely desire.
- ❏ Something you really don't want to happen.
- ❏ Anything that is a substitute for an intimate relationship with God.
- ❏ Something that lifts up you, not God.

Adapted from "How To Hear God's Voice" by Mark and Patty Virkler
Available at www.cwgministries.org
(used with permission)

Find Its Origin, Test Its Content & Check Its Fruit 1 John 4:1,5;
Matthew 7:16

SELF	GOD	ANOTHER SPIRIT
Comes from the mind/a progressive building of ideas. My wants, desires, & thoughts.	Pictures and thoughts come from the inner—most being. Sensed in spirit, then formed.	Comes from the mind. A picture or thought.
May be good or bad. Consideration of things I have learned. May or may not want to test it.	Instructive, uplifting, comforting & peaceful, Not afraid of testing.	Negative, destructive, pushy, fearful, anxious, unsettled, exhaustion, condemnation. Afraid of being tested.
Results vary.	Quickens faith, peace, good fruit, knowledge, enlightenment, strength & humility.	Fear, compulsion, bondage, anxiety, confusion, inflated ego.

SUGGESTED READING

(In no particular order)

The Fourth Dimension by Paul Yonggi Cho © 1979
Bridge Publishing, Inc. Southplainfield, New Jersey

Developing Your Prophetic Gifting by Graham Cooke © 1994
Sovereign World Ltd., Ventura, CA.

Absolute Surrender by Andrew Murray © 1982
Whitaker House, New Kensington, PA.

Abide In Christ by Andrew Murray © 1979
Whitaker House, New Kensington, PA

Experiencing God Through Prayer by Madame Jeanne Guyon © 1984
Whitaker House, Springdale, PA.

The Practice of the Presence of God by Brother Lawrence © 1967
Spire Books, Grand Rapids, MI.

Let Go by Fenelon © 1973
Whitaker, New Kensington, PA.

Gifts of the Spirit by Gordon Lindsay, Volumes 1-4 Reprint 1989
Christ for the Nations, Dallas, TX.

Forever Ruined for the Ordinary by Joy Dawson © 2001
Thomas Nelson Publishers, Nashville, TN.

Numbers In the Bible by Robert D. Johnston
Kregal Publications, Grand Rapids, MI.

Dreams and Visions by Jane Hamon © 2000
Regal Books, Ventura, CA.

Dreams: Wisdom Within by Herman Riffel © 1990
Destiny Image, Shippensburg, PA. 17257

Every Dreamers Handbook by Ira L. Mulligan © 2000
Treasure House, Shippensburg, PA. 17257-0310

Wasted On Jesus by Jim W. Goll © 2000
Destiny Image, Shippensburg, PA. 17257-1319

Unleashing the Power of Praying in the Spirit by Oral Roberts © 1987
Tulsa, Oklahoma 74171

Flying Higher by Rick Godwin © 1999
Creation House, Lake Mary, Florida 32746

Celebration of Discipline by Richard Foster © 1978, 1988, 1998
HarperCollins Publishers, Inc. New York, N.Y. 10022

Experiencing the Depths of Jesus Christ by Jeanne Guyon © CMCMLXXV by
Gene Edwards SeedSowers Christian Books Publishing House, Beaumont,
TX. 77704-3568

Activating the Gifts of the Holy Spirit by David Ireland © 1983
Destiny Image, Shippensburg, PA. 17257

Lord Change Me by Evelyn Christenson © 1993, 1977 by SP Publications,
Inc.
Victor Books, Wheaton, Illinois

Anything by Bill Hamon

Anything by Cindy Jacobs

Anything by Kim Clement

Anything by Lance Wallnau